Greece & Rome

NEW SURVEYS IN THE CLASSICS No. 23

ROMAN VERSE SATIRE

BY

SUSAN H. BRAUND

Published for the Classical Association

OXFORD UNIVERSITY PRESS

1992

Oxford University Press, Walton Street, Oxford OX2 6DP
Oxford New York Toronto
Delhi Bombay Calcutta Madras Karachi
Petaling Jaya Singapore Hong Kong Tokyo
Nairobi Dar Es Salaam Cape Town
Melbourne Auckland
and associated companies in
Berlin Ibadan

ISSN 0017-3835
ISBN 019 922072-7

© Oxford University Press, 1992

Printed in Great Britain
by Bell and Bain Ltd.,
Glasgow

PREFACE

This volume is my personal view of the genre of Roman verse satire, a view shaped by my wise teachers John Henderson and Ted Kenney, by the undergraduates who have attended my classes on the subject during the past ten years and by some of the scholarship published in recent decades. In general, the most important work has been done in the English language, chiefly by scholars working in North America; and, in any case, with the readership of this series in mind, I have largely refrained from citing works in any other language. I have tried to indicate particularly significant works of scholarship by special mention in the text or notes and have simply omitted works which seem misleading or worse. This is not a forum for the intricacies of academic disputation; it is a forum for guidance. All the works cited will be found in the Bibliography at the end. Thanks are due to Niall Rudd for permission to use excerpts from his translations of Horace, Persius, and Juvenal and to Francis Cairns (Publications) for permission to use excerpts from Guy Lee's translation of Persius. I should also like to thank Sue Eames for typing the text and the Librarian of the Joint Library at Gordon Square for supplying books and photocopies.

CONTENTS

I	Approaches to Satire	1
II	Origins	6
III	Lucilius	10
IV	Horace	16
V	Persius	33
VI	Juvenal	40
VII	Overview of the Genre	56
	Bibliography	59

I. APPROACHES TO SATIRE

Satire is . . . ?

Everyone thinks they know what satire is, or, at least, what is meant by 'satire'. But this knowledge is a dangerous thing. It conceals the fact that the term 'satire' has two meanings.[1] For us, it denotes a tone of voice which may occur in virtually any form – a novel, a letter, a play, a cartoon, a comic sketch. But for the Romans it denoted a specific form of literature, the two literary genres of satire, Roman verse satire and prose 'Menippean' satire. Strict rules governed the form and content of these literary genres; these rules emerge from the study of the satires which survive. Yet both genres are recognizable as satire and it is clear that modern theories about the origin and nature of satire apply with equal validity to Roman satire. In this introduction I shall attempt to present a few of the most significant of the modern approaches to satire.

First, it is important to notice that the approaches to satire which are based upon a biographical interpretation, involving the identification of the views expressed in satirical poems with those of the author, and which typically present the satirist as a moral crusader or social reformer are now slowly, and rightly, being rejected in favour of approaches which emphasize the artistic aspect of the satirist's work. Such approaches take satire seriously as poetry and offer analysis of satire as the artistic products of the culture and intellectual milieu of the time, whichever time that might be.[2]

Satire is . . . spells and curses

One very influential view of satire is that of Elliott.[3] He suggests that the origin of satire lies in primitive spells and curses uttered and controlled by a powerful figure in society, such as a witch-doctor or a bard, for the good of society. That is, the primitive equivalent of the satirist had the function of driving out from society the impurities, often embodied in an individual who was made a scapegoat, in order to keep society clean and untainted. Elliott's exposition of the development of literary satire from such highly functional and anthropologically significant beginnings is very persuasive.

Similar is the view of Richlin. She suggests that 'satire is a genre intrinsically concerned with power' and that 'the performance of the satire reinforces the desired social norms'.[4] Satire tends to assume norms and to take as its victims those who deviate from those norms – hence the satire directed against 'out-groups' such as foreigners, women, *nouveaux riches*, and so on.

The power wielded by the words of the satirist figure is clearly very great. So great, in fact, that it tends to inspire a reaction of ambivalence.[5] The audience may be unsure how to respond. Should we approve of the satirist or disapprove? Should we identify with him (and it generally is a 'him') or dissociate ourselves? The answer will vary from audience to audience, from reader to reader. What is certain is that this ambivalence renders satire a challenging and potentially threatening type of literature. It invariably engenders strong reactions.

Satire is . . . drama

Another, complementary, view of satire sees it as a form of drama. This is especially valuable. In the case of Roman satire this analogy reminds us that the satirists wrote their poems for performance, that is, to be recited to an audience, rather than to be read silently. An even more important aspect of the analogy with drama is the introduction of the concept of the mask, or *persona*. Much of the recent work on Roman satire emphasizes that the authors of satire do not utter their own opinions but create a character or mask, *persona*.[6] Understanding of the satirists' use of masks is crucial to an appreciation of Roman satire. It saves us from falling into the trap of biographical interpretation, in which an attempt is made to recreate the events of the poet's life from the poems. Instead, we realize that there is a difference and a distance between the poet and the character he has created. This enables us to examine the character created just as we do a character in a drama. And if we discover flaws and inconsistencies in this character, we should assume that the satirist created them deliberately, for a purpose, and we should try to discover what that purpose is. It is possible that the satirist is inviting us to reject or find fault with the character and his views.

So important is this concept of the *persona* that scholars have tried to find ways to remind readers of the distinction between creator and created. One method is to present the author's name in inverted commas, e.g. 'Horace'. Another is to refer to the character created by the author as 'the speaker'. Both methods are adopted in this volume, as appropriate.

Satire is . . . urban

The setting of the drama enacted in works of satire is predominantly urban.[7] This can be explained simply. The city, because it is a metropolis, a port, or the centre of political power, offers an unrivalled richness of material to the satirist. The city is a melting-pot of people and things: people of all classes and origins and behaviour, things from all over the world and with all kinds of associations. The city is where anything is possible, where any combination of people and things is imaginable. This is what makes the city so attractive to the satirist.

Satire is . . . entertainment

Some of the books on satire, particularly those on Roman satire, suggest that satire is a form of moralizing or philosophy or rhetoric or social history. This ignores the strong element of humour and wit present in all satire, including Roman satire. With contemporary satire, it is, perhaps, less difficult to see the entertainment aspect. With the satire of another culture, this can be more difficult, because it involves an understanding of what might be classed as 'entertainment'. The Roman audience of satire, like that of most other forms of Roman literature, was essentially composed of the élite, men who had enjoyed a high level of literary and rhetorical training in Latin and Greek. For them, entertainment often involved sophisticated allusion to other works of literature and the clever reworking of motifs borrowed from other contexts.[8]

Further, it is important never to forget that Roman verse satire is first and foremost poetry. This was self-evident to the Romans simply from its verse form, despite the (mock-)humility of some of the authors of Roman satire who present their poetry as lowly 'chats'.[9] The metre used in Roman satire is the hexameter, which has been hijacked from the top type of ancient literature, epic poetry. In any recitation of Roman satire, the audience will have been well aware that the metre was that of heroic verse. Moreover, it is clear that the Roman satirists, again despite their own implications to the contrary,[10] organized their satires in books just as did poets working in other genres, such as pastoral, lyric, and elegy.[11] This too indicates a poetic self-consciousness.

Satire is . . . a parasite

One striking feature of the studies of satire is the variety of definitions generated, probably more than for any other type of literature. This in itself should be regarded not as problematic but as characteristic.[12] Satire is a type of literature which derives its material from a much wider range than other genres. This material includes all types of human communication, discourse and literature. This means that satire is essentially parasitic: it continually exploits and re-uses other forms of discourse, both literary and non-literary, always in travesty, parody, or inversion.[13]

Satire is ...

Finally, is it possible to offer one definition of satire superior to the rest? The choice from the many definitions available is wide. But I have discovered none better, as a useful working definition, than that of Feinberg: 'the playfully critical distortion of the familiar'.[14] The value of this four-term definition is that it allows the flexibility necessary to encompass the entire genre. The subject-matter of satire is always 'the familiar', distorted to a greater or lesser extent by satirical devices such as exaggeration, stereotyping, caricature, and inversion. The remaining two terms describe the treatment of that subject-matter. They can be visualized as two sliding scales which make up the axes of a graph. The first is the scale of playfulness. This is another way of referring to the wit and humour, the cleverness and entertainment provided by the satirist. The second is the scale of criticism. This refers to the element of invective in satire, which may vary from fierce, personalized attack on a single individual to milder, more generalized criticism of a fault common in society. In this way, any work of satire can be plotted upon the graph created by these two scales or axes. Some will exhibit marked levels of both playfulness and criticism, others will have one element more strongly than the other.[15] This application of Feinberg's four-term definition makes it possible to reflect the variations between different cultures, different periods, different authors, and even different poems while still providing a recognizable umbrella called 'satire'.

NOTES

1. On the two meanings of 'satire' and for an illuminating essay on the nature of satire see Frye (1944).
2. A good example is Martyn (1979), a study of Juvenal's wit.
3. Elliott (1960).
4. Richlin (1984), 67.
5. On this ambivalence see Kernan (1959), pp. 22–8.
6. There are several useful discussions of the *persona*, including Kernan (1959), pp. 14–30 and on Roman satire Anderson (1982), pp. 3–10, Dessen (1968), pp. 6–9.
7. Hodgart (1969), p. 129 'satire is an urban art', pp. 135–7, Kernan (1959) pp. 7–14, Braund (1989), pp. 23–6.
8. On the centrality of entertainment see Hodgart (1969), p. 12. For an example drawn from Juvenal *Satire* 3 see Braund (1989), pp. 34–6.

9. The characteristic Latin word is *sermones* or *sermo*, used by Lucilius (e.g. 1039 W = 1039 M, 1085 W = 1015 M, 1086 W = 1016 M) and Horace (e.g. *Sat.* I.4.42, *Ep.* II.1.250, II.2.60), cf. Persius 5.14–15.

10. The classic example is Juvenal's use of the phrase 'my volume's hotch-potch' (*farrago libelli*) at 1.86 which may seem to imply a random miscellany. For interpretation of the phrase see Cloud & Braund (1982), pp. 78–9.

11. See Zetzel (1980) on Horace's first book of *Satires* and Cloud & Braund (1982) on Juvenal Book I.

12. Thus Classen (1988) describes it as 'the elusive genre' and suggests (114) that its central characteristic is variety, *varietas*, of forms, contents, and purposes.

13. See Hodgart (1969), pp. 30–2 on the centrality of travesty to satire.

14. Feinberg (1963), p. 7.

15. Frye (1957), pp. 224–5 takes a similar view: 'Two things ... are essential to satire; one is wit or humor founded on fantasy or a sense of the grotesque or absurd, the other is an object of attack. Attack without humor, or pure denunciation, forms one of the boundaries of satire.... The humor of pure fantasy [is] the other boundary of satire.'

II. ORIGINS

The Romans themselves had theories about the origins of the genre of satire and the significance of its name, *satura*.[1] Probably the most famous statement is Quintilian's: 'Satire is entirely our own.'[2] What he meant by that is open to debate; we will return to it at the end of this section.

Apart from Quintilian's comments, we find theory about the genre of *satura* appearing incidentally in the historian Livy's discussion of the history of Roman drama and directly in the writings of Diomedes, a fourth century grammarian. Livy's elaborate theory of the development of Roman drama including a dramatic *satura* is unconvincing and it appears that he is attempting to find a similar pattern of development in Roman drama as existed for Greek drama.[3] Yet we should not overlook one highly significant aspect of his theory. He regards *satura* as an early dramatic form. Not only does this bear out the comments made above concerning the affinity of satire and drama. It also helps explain the links drawn by the satirists themselves between satire and Old Greek Comedy.[4] That satire and drama, in particular comedy, were regarded as closely related genres will prove an important element in the understanding of individual poems.

Our only directly theoretical discussion of the genre of *satura* is that of Diomedes, a fourth-century grammarian who may have derived this material from the polymath Varro, who was writing in the late Republic.[5] Diomedes offers four possible explanations of the word *satura*, all of which reflect certain views of the genre (Diomedes *GLK* I 485):

satura takes its name either from satyrs, because in this form of poetry laughable and disgraceful things are said in the same way as if produced and performed by satyrs; or from a full dish which, stuffed with many varied first-fruits, was offered to the gods in religious ritual among the ancients and was called *satura* from the abundance and fullness of the material; ... or from a certain type of sausage which, stuffed with many ingredients, Varro says was called *satura*.... Others think that its name came from the *lex satura* (lit. 'full law') which combines together many provisions in a single bill, because in the poetry form *satura* many poems are combined together.

The first derivation connects *satura* with satyrs, *Satyri*. This appears to be a reference to the ribald and obscene nature of Greek satyr drama, the type of play staged as an after-piece to tragedies. But the evident implication that Roman satire is similarly obscene does not stand up. What is more, the Greek word *satyros* would produce in Latin the adjective *satyrikos* (as in Petronius' work, *Satyrica*) but not *satura*.

Diomedes' second explanation of *satura* connects it with the *lanx satura*, the 'mixed dish'. This was a plate filled with many different offerings which was presented to the gods at religious festivals. On this theory, the noun *lanx* was dropped leaving the adjective *satura* standing alone. This explanation makes *satura* a metaphor, 'the mixed (dish)', a metaphor which evokes abundance and variety and which suggests that this genre of poetry, as usual in the ancient world, was an offering to the gods. The third explanation is similar to the second: that *satura* designates a kind of stuffing or sausage made from many ingredients. This explanation presents another metaphor of fullness and variety, but of a more mundane nature than the second explanation. Diomedes' fourth suggestion is that *satura* derives from a law, the *lex per saturam*, a law with mixed provisions which we know existed in Republican times. This explanation, like the second and third, again hinges upon the notion of mixture and variety.

We are not in a position to make a firm choice between Diomedes' four explanations, beyond expressing doubts on linguistic grounds about the first.[6] But what is significant is that explanations two, three and four all present satire as a genre of abundance and variety. We are invited to view the genre as the poet's offering of a 'mixed dish' to the inspiring deity; or we can view the poet as acting as a moral legislator on a variety of topics. But it is perhaps most appealing to view the satirist as a cook, serving up to his audience a sausage stuffed full of varied ingredients – including, incidentally, a substantial quantity of feasting and food! This explanation at least gives a piquant taste to Juvenal's description of his work as a *farrago* (1.86): by styling his poetry as 'mixed cattle fodder' he may very well be debunking the theory of the origin of the word *satura*.

Theories of the origin of the word *satura* must remain guess-work. But Diomedes' introductory comments on the nature of the genre and its practitioners are most helpful (*GLK* I 485):

Satire is the name of the Roman form of poetry that is nowadays abusive and composed to criticize the vices of men in the manner of Old Comedy, such as was written by Lucilius and Horace and Persius; but formerly satire was the name given to the form of poetry made up of a variety of poems, such as was written by Pacuvius and Ennius.[7]

Immediately striking is the link with Old Greek Comedy, which connects with the remarks above about the close interrelationship between satire and drama. Equally striking is his division of the genre historically into, on the one hand, the form written by Lucilius, Horace, and Persius and, on the other hand, the older form written by Pacuvius and Ennius. Quintilian similarly names Lucilius, Horace, and Persius as the chief exponents of the genre (Juvenal dates from a little later):

> The first to win renown in *satura* was Lucilius who has some fans who are so dedicated to him that they without hesitation prefer him not just to other authors in the same genre but to all poets. I disagree with them as much as with Horace, who thinks that Lucilius is a muddy river with a lot of stuff that you could remove. Remarkable is his learning and his freedom of speech and the sharpness and abundant wit which derives from it. Much terser and purer is Horace and, unless I lapse because of my affection for him, the best. Persius has won a considerable and legitimate reputation, although he wrote only one book. There are eminent satirists today who will be celebrated in the future. (*Institutio Oratoria* 10.1.93–4)

Lucilius, it is clear, was regarded both by theorists and by the satirists themselves as the founder of the genre; most memorably Horace calls him its 'inventor' at *Satires* I.10.48.

But where does this leave Ennius and his nephew Pacuvius, mentioned by Diomedes? And what does Quintilian mean by claiming that 'Satire is entirely our own'? Nothing is known of Pacuvius' works. Quintus Ennius (239–169 B.C.), his uncle, was from Calabria in the south of Italy and hence was influenced by the cultures of Greece, Italy, and Rome.[8] This multiculturalism manifested itself in the literary innovations made by Ennius. Of prime importance is his establishment of the form of Latin epic poetry in his *Annals* (*Annales*). The nature of his Satires, *Saturae*, is difficult to judge because only 31 lines survive from the four books he wrote.[9] But it appears that Ennius' *Saturae* were a real miscellany written in a variety of metres. One fragment (28–31 W) consists of a multiple word-play on the words *frustra* and *frustrari*, while another presents personifications of the abstract in a debate between Life and Death (Quintilian *I.O.* 9.2.36), while yet another presents a fable of Aesop (preserved by Aulus Gellius 2.29). A critical tone is present in the fragment which compares human beings with monkeys (23 W: 'the monkey – how similar to us is that most disgusting beast') and humour combined with autobiographical presentation is evident in fragment 21 W: 'I never write poetry except when gouty'. This is not much to go on. We have to accept the judgement of the ancients in pronouncing Lucilius and not Ennius the inventor of the genre of satire.[10] Some possible reasons for this will be discussed below in the section on Lucilius.

Finally, we return to the significance of Quintilian's comment about satire. This has been interpreted in two different ways. Firstly, to mean that there is no original Greek form which the Roman satirists are imitating.[11] Secondly, to mean that the Roman satirists are so completely superior to Greek satirists that they win hands down and do not permit Quintilian even to mention any Greek satirists by name.[12] In assessing these interpretations, it is crucial to bear in mind the context of Quintilian's comments. In this part of his *Institutio Oratoria* he is prescribing the ideal components of the school syllabus, with a view to selecting the very best elements of Greek and Latin literature for a Roman school-child to read and study. He divides up his material into Greek authors and Roman authors and proceeds through a genre-by-genre evaluation of the relative merits of different authors. When he reaches satire, he mentions no Greek original of Roman verse satire, nor are we aware of the existence of any such. Of course, there are satirical passages in Greek authors writing in other genres, but there was no Greek satire in the form used by Lucilius, Horace, and Persius.[13] Thus it seems that the first interpretation of Quintilian's statement is correct: Quintilian is indeed claiming originality – and, it simply follows, superiority – for the Romans in the genre of Roman satire.

NOTES

1. For modern discussions see van Rooy (1965), pp. 1–29, Knoche (1975), pp. 3–16, Coffey (1989), pp. 3–23.
2. Quintilian, *Institutio Oratoria* 10.1.93: *satura quidem tota nostra est*.
3. Into his account of the development of Roman drama Livy incorporates a dramatic form which he names *satura*, which designates a musical stageshow without an organized plot. See Coffey (1989), pp. 18–22 and 274 for quotation and discussion of the passage (Livy 7.2.4–10); both Coffey and Gratwick (1982), pp. 160–2 reject the hypothesis of a dramatic *satura*.
4. Horace *Satires* I.4.1–5, I.10.16, Persius 1.123–4.
5. Marcus Terentius Varro, 116–27 B.C. It is a great regret that neither his *De compositione saturarum* nor his four books of *Saturae* survive. On the likely influence of Varro on Diomedes see van Rooy (1965), pp. 1–4 and notes for further bibliography.
6. See van Rooy (1965), pp. 1–29 and Coffey (1989), pp. 11–18 for a fuller treatment of Diomedes' discussion of *satura*.
7. *satura dicitur carmen apud Romanos nunc quidem maledicum et ad carpenda hominum uitia archaeae comoediae charactere compositum, quale scripserunt Lucilius et Horatius et Persius; sed olim carmen quod ex uariis poematibus constabat satura uocabatur, quale scripserunt Pacuuius et Ennius*.
8. His statement that he had 'three hearts' (*tria corda*) probably means that he was fluent in Greek, Latin, and Oscan, the language of southern Italy at that time. On Ennius' multiculturalism see Coffey (1989), pp. 25–7.
9. The standard text of Ennius is that of Vahlen (1963). The fragments of the *Satires* are most readily available in Warmington (1956) (*Remains of Old Latin Vol.* 1, Loeb Classical Library) on pages 384–95.
   For a brief overview see Gratwick (1982), pp. 158–60; for fuller discussion see van Rooy (1965), pp. 30–49, Ramage, Sigsbee & Fredericks (1974), pp. 12–21, Knoche (1975), pp. 17–30 and Coffey (1989), pp. 24–32 with notes for further bibliography.
10. Whereas Ennius is described by Horace as 'the author of a crude verse never handled by the Greeks' (*Satires* 1.10.66).
11. The line of Horace where he calls satire 'verse never handled by the Greeks' (*Satires* I.10.66 *Graecis intacti carminis*) seems to support Quintilian's view.
12. See Gratwick (1982), pp. 160–2 for a succinct summary of the debate and van Rooy (1965), pp. 117–23 for a fuller discussion, including helpful tabulation of material in Quintilian *I.O.* 10.1.
13. Closest is iambic poetry, such as that of Archilochus, Hipponax and Callimachus. For surveys of some satiric elements in Greek literature see van Rooy (1965), pp. 90–116, Witke (1970), pp. 21–48 and on Callimachus' *Iambs* Dawson (1950).

III. LUCILIUS

Gaius Lucilius died at Naples in 102/1 B.C. as an old man. He was born probably in 180 B.C., or possibly 168/7 B.C., into an eminent, rich family of the Latin aristocracy in Campania. Lucilius was almost certainly educated at Rome and owned large estates in southern Italy and Sicily and an important house in Rome. He was an *eques* (cavalryman: the second highest social class), a friend of the great general and politician Scipio Aemilianus, a patron of the arts around whom gathered a group of intellectuals, including poets and philosophers. From about 130 B.C. onwards Lucilius wrote his *Satires*, in a total of thirty books of which only 1300 fragments survive.[1] Most of these are very brief and can hardly be considered a representative sample, since the vast majority were preserved by later grammarians as examples of oddities of Latin linguistic usage.

Lucilius' high social status, as a member of the Latin aristocracy and as a friend of Scipio Aemilianus, gave him the freedom to attack eminent men in his *Satires*. Moreover, it appears that Scipio (like his grandfather, Scipio Africanus, two generations earlier) wished to foster the best in Latin literature. In this atmosphere, Lucilius took the genre which Ennius had handled and in the course of his poetic career he established the chief characteristics of Roman *satura*.[2] For this reason, Lucilius was rightly regarded as the 'inventor' of the genre (Horace *Satires* I.10.48).

In his earliest books of *Satires*, numbered 26–30, Lucilius followed Ennius' example of writing in a variety of metres, chiefly the metres of drama (iambo-trochaic metres), until Book 30, which is entirely in hexameters. Books 1–21 establish the hexameter as the metre of the genre; of Books 22–25, which use the elegiac metre, little survives and less is known of their date or place in Lucilius' output.[3] It is perhaps surprising that the metre of epic poetry – the highest genre of poetry, which recorded the inspiring exploits of heroes, kings and generals – was hijacked for a genre of starkly contrasting mundane content and critical tone. A partial precedent for this may be found in the re-handling of traditional epic themes by the Greek Hellenistic poets who chose to emphasize non-heroic and even mundane aspects of mythology (for example, Callimachus in his *Hecale* and Theocritus in *Idyll* 13). Further, it is evident that the element of parody of epic poetry is prominent in Roman satire. But these two factors only go a little way towards explaining the radical nature of

Lucilius' use of the hexameter. The inherent conflict between form and content must have been striking to the Roman ear.

It is hard to reconstruct the content of the books of Lucilius' *Satires*. Some evidently contained a medley of several short poems, thus continuing Ennius' type of *satura*, while others consisted of a single, longer poem. It is clear that he used a variety of forms in his poems, including monologue, dialogue and the letter. Monologue is possibly the most prevalent form adopted by Lucilius, although the fragmentary preservation of his poems makes that hard to judge. Dialogue seems in evidence in Lucilius' earliest book, where he receives advice from a friend or interlocutor (713–14 W = 620–1 M; echoed in Horace *Satires* II.1.10–11), and from some of the fragments of Book 30, which indicate a debate between Lucilius and his critics. In this poem, Lucilius is evidently criticized for the ferocity of his attacks and responds to these criticisms:[4] e.g. 1085 W (= 1015 M): 'You enjoy publishing widely in your discourses those bad reports about me'; 1079–80 W (= 1022–3 M): 'This man, like set mouse-traps, like a scorpion with tail upraised'; and 1081 W (= 1018 M): 'This man on the ground in the dung and filth of the sty and the pig-shit'. The letter form is most obvious in Book 3, in the description of a journey from Rome to Sicily, for example, 102–5 W (= 110–13 M):

> But there this was play and everything was free and easy,
> all this I say was free and easy, play and fun;
> but that was hard work, when we reached the boundary of Setia,
> goat-deserted mountains, all Etnas, rugged Athoses

and 109–10 W (= 117–18 M): 'This Bovillan jut-mouth with his one little sticking-out tooth is a rhinoceros'. Lines 186–8 W (= 181–3 M) are also clearly from an epistle:

> I will tell you how I am, although you do not ask,
> since I have managed to stay among the number in which the majority
> of mankind is not found.

All three forms appear in subsequent Roman Satire.

In terms of content, too, Lucilius established the repertoire of the genre. Most striking, in contrast with Ennius, is Lucilius' criticism of individuals. He attacks both eminent men and the more lowly for a variety of faults ranging from incompetence to arrogance.[5] This was the essence of his reputation.[6] Criticisms of elements of what may loosely be termed 'everyday life' feature prominently. His portrayal of the hustle and bustle of city life is one which finds parallels through the ages (1145–51 W = 1228–34 M):

> But as it is from morning to night, on holiday and workday,
> the whole people and senators too all alike
> are bustling about the Forum and nowhere leave off;
> they all devote themselves to one and the same pursuit and expertise –
> to be able to swindle successfully, to fight cunningly,
> to compete in flattery, to pretend to be an upright citizen,
> to lay ambushes as if everyone were everyone's enemies.

Feasting and drinking take a prominent part in the fragments, ranging from moralizing about excessive consumption (1022–3 W = 1073–4 M):

> For you know well that in wine there lies a lingering illness
> for mortals when a person has entertained himself too richly

to the descriptions of lavish dinners,[7] e.g. 601–3 W (= 1174–6 M):

> Besides he ordered each person's desire to be made and brought to the table.
> This man was drawn to pigs' udders and a dish of fattened fowls,
> the other to a licker-fish of the Tiber caught between the two bridges.

Morality, philosophy, and religion are other themes which appear in the *Satires*. The first is exemplified in the longest fragment of Lucilius which survives, the so-called *Virtus* fragment (1196–1208 W = 1326–8 M):[8]

> Excellence, Albinus, is being ready to pay what is truly due
> in our business dealings and in life's affairs;
> excellence is knowing what each matter involves for a person;
> excellence is knowing what is right, useful, and honourable,
> what things are good and what are bad, what is useless, shameful, and dishonourable;
> excellence is knowing the end and limit of acquiring an object;
> excellence is the ability to pay what is due to riches;
> excellence is giving what is truly owed to honour,
> being an enemy and no friend of bad people and conduct,
> and on the other hand being a defender of good people and conduct,
> valuing highly the latter, wishing them well, being a life-long friend to them;
> and besides thinking first of the interests of our country,
> then of our parents' interests, thirdly and lastly of our own.

It has been suggested that this 'advice' is aimed ironically at an Albinus who had behaved less than excellently.[9] There is parody of Stoic ideas at 1189–90 W (= 1225–6 M) and philosophical ideas misapplied for comic effect at 805–11 W (784–90 M). Another fragment criticizes the superstitious (524–9 W = 484–9 M):

> At scarecrows and witches, which were established by the Fauni
> and Numae Pompilii, this man trembles and thinks them all-important.

> As baby children believe that all bronze statues
> are alive and are people, so these think that the fictions of dreams
> are real, they believe that in the bronze statues there is a heart.
> These are a painter's gallery, nothing real, all make-believe.

Questions of literature are not confined to the debate between Lucilius and his critics in Book 30 (above). In 401–10 W (= 338–47 M) he considers the essence of unity of large-scale poems like Ennius' *Annals* or the *Iliad* in a reflection of current Hellenistic theory on this matter. On a smaller scale, Lucilius also pronounces upon matters of spelling, e.g. 394–5 W (= 375–6 M) and 384–7 W (= 358–61 M).

But what is most notable about Lucilius, apart from his fierce invective, is the distinctive autobiographical presentation of the *Satires*, frequently with a marked element of criticism and irony at his own expense. Horace draws attention to this characteristic of Lucilius' work at *Satires* II.1.30–34 (cf. II.1.71–4):

> In the past he would confide his secrets to his books, which he trusted
> like friends; and whether things went well or badly he'd always
> turn to them; in consequence, the whole of the old man's life
> is laid before us, as if it were painted on a votive tablet.

Thus he says (650–1 W = 671–2 M):
> But that I should become a tax-gatherer in Asia, an assessment-man
> instead of Lucilius, that I refuse, and I would not exchange everything
>   for this alone.

The self-irony emerges in fragments such as 1183 W (= 1248 M), if this is indeed spoken by Lucilius in the first person: 'I wetted the bed right through and made messes on the skins'; more securely, in 635 W (= 592–3 M), his statement of his preferred audience – not the high-brow intellectual but the average educated man: 'I don't care for Persius to read me but I do want Decimus Laelius to'; and in the ways he refers to his poetry at 1039 W (= 1039 M) 'our play and chats' and at 1131 W (= 1279 M) 'I who make ramshackle poetry' where the Greek word *schedium* denotes an impromptu poem or speech. Lucilius' autobiographical presentation and in particular his self-irony were especially significant influences upon later satirists.[10] It is important when considering Lucilius' self-presentation to realize that, like the later Roman satirists, he presents a multifaceted *persona*, at times the humble poet, at others the cynic preacher or the buffoon.

To match this mundane subject-matter and humble stance, Lucilius adopts an informal, unelevated style of diction, called 'thin' (*gracilis*) by

Varro.[11] Some of his language is not only frank but obscene and explicit. For example, 354–5 W (= 331–2 M): 'because he is a deformed, rheumaticky, gouty old man, because he is a maimed, lanky wretch with a big rupture'; 1081 W cited above; 1183 W cited above; and particularly in his descriptions of women and sex.[12] A conversational flavour, highly suited to his styling of his poems as *sermones*, 'chats',[13] is generated in particular by a certain repetitiveness and looseness of structure, illustrated well by 102–5 W above. It is instructive that Horace criticizes Lucilius for a lack of stylistic polish and looseness of composition (e.g. *Satires* I.4.9–13, I.10.50–64), although he concedes that for his time he exhibits a high level of sophistication (*Satires* I.10.64–71). Fronto describes another feature of Lucilius' diction, that he drew on 'the technical words in every art and business'.[14] A further distinctive feature is his use of Greek words: although the effect of this varies according to context, it in general reflects the blending of Greek and Roman culture during the second century B.C. One striking, fierce line consists of just four words, two in Latin and two compounded of Greek words (1048 W = 1058 M): *inberbi androgyni, barbati moechocinaedi*, 'beardless she-males, bearded sodom-adulterers'. Another instance of the use of Greek, this time for the purpose of witty entertainment, is where Lucilius uses a quotation from Homer for allusive, humorous effect (267–8 W = 231–2 M): 'so that it be no different than if "Apollo snatched him away"'. At the other end of the scale are cases of epic parody, for example in Book 1 where he models a scene of the council of the gods on Book 1 of Ennius' *Annales*.[15]

His use of parody underlines the fact that Lucilius was an educated man writing for an educated audience, that could and would detect and enjoy such parody. As such, he is very much a product of his time and place. He reflects the interests, ideals, and aspirations of the men with whom he consorted, in particular Scipio Aemilianus, more often by exposing failure to attain these ideals than by overt articulation of the principles.[16] This is epitomized graphically in Horace's portrayal of Lucilius at *Satires* II.1.62–74:

> When Lucilius first had the courage
> to write this kind of poetry and remove the glossy skin
> in which people were parading before the world and concealing
> their ugliness, was Laelius offended by his wit or the man who rightly
> took on the name of the African city which he overthrew?
> Or did they feel any pain when Metellus was wounded and Lupus
> was smothered in a shower of abusive verse? And yet Lucilius
> indicted the foremost citizens and the whole populace, tribe
> by tribe, showing indulgence only to Worth and her friends.

Why, when the worthy Scipio and the wise and gentle Laelius
left the stage of public life for the privacy of home,
they would let their hair down and join the poet in a bit of horseplay,
as they waited for the greens to cook.

He blends a profound knowledge of Greek culture with Roman ideology and is aptly described by Cicero as 'an educated and highly civilized man' (*De orat.* 3.171: *homo doctus et perurbanus*). The striking vigour, bluntness, and aggression of Lucilius' *Satires* are not incompatible with Cicero's words of praise: Cicero approves of his forceful assertion of Roman ideology.

NOTES

1. The most important editions of the text of Lucilius are those of Marx (1904–5) and Warmington (1979); the latter, in the Loeb Classical Library (*Remains of Old Latin Vol.* 3) provides English translation, brief notes, and concordances of cross-references to the edition of Marx.
   The general books on Roman Satire provide excellent surveys of Lucilius: Ramage, Sigsbee & Fredericks (1974), pp. 27–52; Knoche (1975), pp. 31–52; Coffey (1989), pp. 35–62 with notes and pp. 282–3; for further bibliography Christes (1972). For a brief but pithy overview of Lucilius see Gratwick (1982); also Rudd (1986), pp. 2–11, 40–51, 82–9, 126–32, 162–70 with lively translations of the lines cited. General studies include Fiske (1920) on Lucilius' influence on Horace; Puelma-Piwonka (1949) on the characteristics of Lucilius' *sermo* and the relationship with Callimachus' *Iambs*; and Martyn (1966) on Lucilius' imagery.
2. See van Rooy (1965), pp. 51–5.
3. On the arrangement, dating, and metres of Lucilius' books see Gratwick (1982), pp. 168–70 and, on the early books, Raschke (1979).
4. Griffith (1970), esp. pp. 65–72.
5. See Gratwick (1982), p. 163 for a list of the important men attacked by Lucilius and 164 for some of the faults satirized.
6. Thus his successors in the genre portray him as raging against or even physically attacking his victims: Horace *Satires* I.10.3–4: [Lucilius] 'is praised . . . for scouring the city with caustic wit'; *Satires* II.1.62–70 e.g. 'a shower of abusive verse'; Persius 1.114–15: 'Lucilius crunched the city – Lupus and Mucius and all – and smashed his molar'; Juvenal 1.19–20 and 165–6: 'Whenever, as though with sword in hand, the hot Lucilius roars in wrath . . .'.
7. On feasts in Lucilius and other authors of Roman Satire see Shero (1923); for Lucilius' influence upon Horace in the description of *cenae* see Fiske (1920), pp. 408–15.
8. Raschke (1990) rightly observes that *uirtus* here represents an aristocratic ideal rather than a philosophical concept.
9. For possible identifications of Albinus see Gratwick (1982), p. 163, Raschke (1990), pp. 365–9.
10. For example, the phrase 'Socratic pamphlets' (*Socratici charti* 789 W = 710 M), if it refers to his own poetry, suggests the use of dialogue and a self-ironic stance; the phrase is repeated by Horace at *Ars poetica* 310 (*Socraticae . . . chartae*).
11. Cited by Gellius *N.A.* 6.14.6, cf. Fronto p.113 N.
12. For new appraisals of Lucilius on women see Richlin (1983), pp. 164–74, Henderson (1989a), pp. 99–102 and, in more detail, (1989b), pp. 54–7.
13. E.g. 1039 W (= 1039 M), 1085 W (= 1015 M), 1086 W (= 1016 M).
14. Fronto p.62 N.
15. See 30–2 W (= 33–5 M), 19–22 W (= 26–9 M), 35 W (= 31 M), 10 W (= 10 M), 15 W (= 15 M), discussed briefly by Gratwick (1982), pp. 169–70.
16. Raschke (1987), p. 318 is right to describe Lucilius' poetry as 'highly partisan satirical verse'.

IV. HORACE

Although Horace's origins were relatively humble in comparison with those of Lucilius, he rose to high status through wealth and powerful backing. The usual picture of the poor tradesman's son admitted to aristocratic company for his literary genius should be dismissed, as Armstrong powerfully argues.[1] Quintus Horatius Flaccus was born in 65 B.C. at Venusia in Apulia to a freedman (a former slave). His father was an auctioneer (*coactor*, that is, in effect, a type of entrepreneur) and, being very wealthy and ambitious for his son, took him to Rome to ensure that he received a good education. Horace completed his education by spending a year or two in Athens, the university for young Romans of the élite and a very costly experience. It was at Athens that Horace joined the retinue of Brutus, the assassin of Julius Caesar, in 44 B.C. The following year, Brutus appointed Horace *tribunus militum*, tribune of the soldiers, an appointment which carried with it equestrian status. But at the battle of Philippi, late in 42 B.C., Brutus' army was routed and Brutus committed suicide. Horace sustained a further blow to his ambitions on his return home when he discovered a change in his economic circumstances, probably the confiscation of some of his land. He then took the shrewd step of acquiring the post of *scriba quaestorii*, a permanent appointment as assistant to the annually-changing quaestors with responsibility for public finances and public records. This post offered considerable influence and considerable income. Subsequently his friendship with Virgil led in 38 B.C. to an introduction to Maecenas, a rich and influential patron, and then to Octavian, the future emperor; he enjoyed the patronage of Maecenas, epitomized most famously in the gift of the Sabine farm, for the rest of his life. This patronage confirmed his position and influence in society and he repaid the obligation in his poetic output.[2] Later Octavian, now the emperor Augustus, invited him to become his secretary to assist with private correspondence, an offer which Horace declined, itself an indication of the friendly relations he enjoyed with Augustus. When he died in 8 B.C., shortly after Maecenas, he named the emperor as his heir and was buried near Maecenas on the Esquiline.

The first book of *Satires* was his earliest publication, in 35–4 B.C. This was followed by the second book of *Satires* and the book of *Epodes* soon after the Battle of Actium, in 30–29 B.C. *Odes* I–III were published together in 23 B.C. He returned to the hexameter form to publish *Epistles* I in 20–19 B.C. and *Epistles* II.2 the following year. Particularly important is his *Secular Hymn* (*carmen saeculare*), the poem commissioned by Augustus for his celebration of the Secular Games in 17 B.C. In 13 B.C. Horace returned to lyric metres, publishing *Odes* IV.[3] His remaining works, *Epistles* II.1 and so-called *Ars poetica*, are hard to date.[4]

Horace himself categorizes his poetic output into three divisions, saying that it is impossible to please everyone equally (*Epistles* II.2.59–60):

> You put lyric poetry first – he's for iambics –
> *he* prefers the tangy wit of Bion's homilies.

By lyric poetry he means his poems in lyrics metres (*Odes* and the *carmen saeculare*); iambics designates his book of *Epodes*, written in the iambographic tradition of the Greek poet Archilochus; and 'the tangy wit of Bion's homilies' (*Bioneis sermonibus et sale nigro*) designates his writings in the genre of *satura*, that is *Satires* I and II and *Epistles* I and II.[5] Of these, we are concerned only with the third category; although Horace's *Epodes* contain much invective and satirical material, their metre determines that they are a separate genre with a different literary history from Roman hexameter *satura*.[6]

Satires I

In his first book of *Satires*,[7] Horace adopts the autobiographical mode of Lucilius but presents a character whose personality and circumstances change through the course of the book. That is, *Satires* I tells a story. We should not, however, be tempted to read this story as autobiographical self-revelation. Clearly the character has much in common with Quintus Horatius Flaccus, but the poet is using his *persona* to explore wide-ranging ideas about friendship, freedom, power, and literature in a carefully structured way which does not necessarily constitute a diary of the author's experiences.[8]

Zetzel in his seminal article on Book I of the *Satires* has argued powerfully that we should read the poems in the sequence in which Horace arranged them and not plucked from their context.[9] The naming of Maecenas in the opening line of I.1 dedicates the book to him. The issue raised there immediately is people's discontent with their lot. This issue is explored in relation to the specific theme of avarice in a variety of ways during the rest of the poem, through argument interwoven with types drawn from the rhetorical tradition (the soldier, merchant, lawyer, and farmer of lines 4–12), an animal analogy (the ant 32–5), the vignette of the Athenian miser (64–7), the mythological example of Tantalus (68–9) and the anecdote of Ummidius (95–100). Both the theme and its treatment are typical of the Hellenistic diatribe, a form of popular philosophy, something like a sermon, used by many adherents of different philosophical schools from the third century B.C. onwards, of whom Bion of Borysthenes is one of the best known.[10] It seems, then, that in this poem Horace is playing the part of a street-corner preacher, delivering popular wisdom to anyone who will listen, in the tradition of Bion. This view is substantiated by Horace's own characterization of his satirical works as *Bioneis sermonibus* at *Epistles* II.2.60 (quoted above). The essential differences lie in the artifice involved (this is not a Greek sermon in prose but a carefully wrought poem in Latin hexameters), and in the lack of adherence to any single philosophical school.[11]

The same pattern appears in *Sat.* I.2. The general theme, again one familiar from Hellenistic diatribe, is articulated at line 24: 'In avoiding *one* sort of fault fools rush into its opposite,' that is, the lack of and need for a golden mean. The specific topic which Horace uses to illustrate this is sexual conduct and he does so using obscenity, which seems designed to impart a tone of frankness.[12] Again, features characteristic of the Hellenistic diatribe abound: the reference to a well-known comic play (20–2), the use of an interlocutor (23), the quotation from a famous man, here Cato (31–5), the parody of Ennius (37),[13] the personification of Nature (73–4), the illustration of the sheiks (86–9), quotation of direct speech (120) and the picture of the adulterer caught in the act (127–33) which may be drawn from contemporary mime.[14] Again the diatribist created by Horace here belongs to no one philosophical school, although the Cynic attitude to sex is represented strongly,[15] and he delivers no startling new wisdom.

The 'Diatribes of Book I' are completed by the third poem, which shares many features with I.1 and I.2 but also lays the foundations for a shift into a new phase of the 'story'.[16] The general theme of I.3 is human inconsistency and it is illustrated by reference to the conduct of friendship. Again, features of the diatribe mark the speaker as a popular philosopher, e.g. the use of an interlocutor (19, 126), the personification of Reason (78), Expediency (98), and Nature (113), the many named examples in the poem, the reference to mythology (107), the animal analogy (110), the vignette of the boys mocking the philosopher (133–6). What is unusual – and significant – is the emphasis upon friendship in this poem. Friendship will prove to be a major preoccupation throughout Horace's satirical writing. He introduces the topic here by stating his ideal of the kind and tolerant friend who judges fairly his friend's faults. This topic of the fairness (or otherwise) of criticism is, obviously, highly relevant to satire and also to contemporary politics.[17] And in this discussion of friendship he uses himself, ironically and disingenuously, as an example of an inconsiderate chatterbox (63–4)[18] and encourages Maecenas to consider him 'rather uninhibited'! This detail makes the issue of friendship highly specific: it is friendship with the great and powerful, the conduct required of those admitted into Maecenas' clique, which particularly interests Horace. This will remain the central topic of Book I.

If in I.3 Horace portrays himself as on the periphery of Maecenas' circle, in I.4 he starts to present his credentials for acceptance, in this fictionalized version of his upwards mobility. As his literary credentials, he indicates that he is following Lucilius' practice of criticizing people's faults, though not Lucilius' style, which he condemns for its verbosity (9–13).[19] He defends himself against the charge of malice, so readily brought against satirists, by denying that he can be considered a poet (39–42) and that he is ever malevolent (78–103). He goes on to concede that if he is frank (*liberius* 103, picking up the 'fault' claimed in I.3) this is due to the moral education he received from his father (105–29).[20] In this way he marries his literary credentials with his moral credentials, claiming an exemplary intent for his Lucilian frankness, *libertas*.[21] *Satires* I.4 is a manifesto of 'Horace's' worth.

The next poem further develops the themes of I.4. It affirms Horace's choice of and debt to Lucilius as a model, for the poem with its diary-like 'autobiographical' account of Horace's journey to Brundisium is clearly closely based upon Lucilius' satire portraying a journey to Sicily.[22] At first sight, this poem appears to be the simplest of poems: the straightforward telling of a journey, full of mundane circumstantial detail and plenty of irony at Horace's own expense (e.g. he portrays his laziness 5, impatience 8, illnesses 7–8, 30–1, 49, naïveté 82–3). But appearances can be deceptive. The poem is, more importantly, a celebration of friendship,[23] friendship with members of Maecenas' circle – Plotius, Varius, and Virgil, for whom Horace professes deep affection (40–2, 93); he does not yet appear to be close to the great man himself. More than this, Horace continues to establish his credentials for acceptance by subtly showing an understanding and sharing of the 'rules' of the group. This accounts for the superior attitude exhibited by the urban, urbane group of friends towards the bumpkins (51–70: the epic parody here emphasizes the superciliousness of the spectators) and anxious-to-please officials (71–6) whom they meet on the journey. But even more significant is Horace's display of discretion. The journey which he describes so 'realistically' was, it is agreed, a political mission on which Maecenas was sent in 37 B.C. to attempt to reconcile Mark Antony with Octavian.[24] The sole indication in the poem of such immense political events is at lines 27–9:

> This was where the excellent Maecenas was due to come,
> along with Cocceius; both were envoys on a mission of immense
> importance; both were adept at reconciling friends who had quarrelled.

Horace's account is in fact highly selective, as if to offer proof of his reliability.

Satires I.6 begins the second half of the book with a rededication to Maecenas in the first line. This is highly appropriate because this poem tells of Horace's acceptance into the charmed circle, in the central passage in the poem (56–64). The remainder of the poem combines tributes to Maecenas for valuing an individual's worth over his birth (1–6, 45–52) with emphatic declarations of Horace's humility (45–6) and satisfaction with his lot (89–92) and a further statement of his moral credentials, which, as in I.4, he attributes to the upbringing he received from his father (71–88).[25]

The book has now risen to an important climax in its story: the popular preacher figure portrayed in the triad I.1–I.3 has developed into the poet who enters the exclusive circle of Maecenas in the 'autobiographical' triad I.4–I.6. Consequently, the next two or three poems have often been regarded as an interlude. While it is clear that the non-autobiographical mode of I.7 and I.8 introduces a lighter tone into the book, to regard these poems as make-weights, inserted simply to bring the number of poems up to ten, is now discredited. Rather, *Satires* I.7–I.9 should be seen as a third triad,[26] in which Horace explores different modes of conflict and the resolution of conflict, a topic introduced earlier in the book most obviously in the slanging-match between Messius and Sarmentus which so entertained Maecenas' coterie in *Satires* I.5 (lines 51–70: the centrepiece of that poem). I.7 takes the form of an anecdote in mock-heroic tone portraying a court case between a man who uses obscene abuse and a man who uses witty ridicule.[27] The fact that the latter wins (or so we must presume, for he has the last word) symbolizes the potency of humour against invective.[28] This seems to be a concrete illustration of Horace's stated preference for joking rather than malice, expressed at I.4.91–103 and perhaps most famously (commencing *ridiculum acri fortius* . . .) at I.10.14–15:

> Humour is often stronger
> and more effective than sharpness in cutting knotty issues.

Satires I.8 also functions on a symbolic level.[29] Superficially, it is a tale told by a wooden statue of the god Priapus of his failure to protect the garden he is supposed to be guarding from invasion by two witches for magic purposes, until he emits a fart which splits his wooden buttocks and scares off the witches. Symbolically, it seems significant that the gardens here are the gardens of Maecenas on the Esquiline and that their would-be guardian invites our laughter at his own expense on account of his helplessness. These features recur more explicitly in the next poem. Possibly Priapus' fart has a similar role to the pun which gained victory in I.7 and can be regarded as a symbol for Horace's type of satire, which uses not malice and spite but ridicule and laughter.[30]

Satires I.9 re-enacts the event of I.8[31] in a return to the autobiographical mode. Horace depicts himself wretchedly assailed by an intruder, usually known as 'The Pest'. The Pest is a social climber who wants Horace to engineer an introduction to Maecenas (43–8). Like Priapus in I.8, Horace seems helpless – he is unable to take an aggressive enough stance – but is saved by a chance miracle (74–8), which he celebrates with the epic allusion which ends the poem.[32] Both the allusion to Homer and the military language throughout portray the incident as a battle.[33] If I.7 and I.8 in some way represent modes of satire, I.9 also celebrates again the standards of Maecenas' circle and the exclusivity of the group, for example in lines 48–9:

> We don't behave up there in the way you imagine. Why nowhere
> is cleaner and more remote from that kind of corruption.

Not only does the Pest manifestly fail to conform to the standards required (although he is evidently blissfully ignorant of this!) but Horace portrays the humorous consequences of the politeness and indirection which he has learned.[34] The poem derives further piquancy from the reflection that earlier in 'the story' Horace himself might have been viewed as an intruder and a social climber.

The final poem draws together and further modifies the most important themes of the book. *Satires* I.10 returns to the issue of Lucilius and his faults raised in I.4. Horace refines his assessment of the man he is glad to call the inventor of the genre (line 48) with a blend of praise and criticism. From this emerges a picture of the qualities valued by Horace: terseness (9), appropriate variation of style (11–14), humour (14–17), and linguistic purity (20–35).[35] This is Horace's poetic manifesto – and, we can presume, it was one designed to find favour with his audience. He presents himself as a 'New Lucilius', not simply in literary terms but also for political motives, to associate Maecenas' circle with the Republican ideal of *libertas*.[36] What is more, Horace concludes the poem, and the book, with a picture of his (ideal) audience, a small, select audience of like-minded friends. With his list of thirteen names, including Maecenas and prominent members of his coterie (81–6), he completes the story of the book, the development from outsider to insider. Thus he reinforces the values and exclusivity of the group into which he has been admitted, as DuQuesnay has shown in his penetrating study.[37] It is difficult to know the extent to which the 'story' of *Satires* I corresponds to 'reality', but we can be confident that this seal (*sphragis*) to the book would have won the approval of those here named, even if outsiders like ourselves are struck by the image of smug self-satisfaction projected in the book.[38]

The linear path taken in this overview cannot do justice to the other manifestations of artistry and sophistication of conception and arrangement in Horace's book of *Satires*. Clearly, Virgil's book of *Eclogues*, published only a few years earlier to great acclamation, was a profound influence.[39] The abundant literature on Horace contains much further elucidation of the patterns of the *Liber Sermonum*[40] and of the wit, humour, and irony of the book.[41]

Satires II

In *Satires* I Horace occupies the stage alone and has us focus upon his *persona* as he tells his 'story' and thereby portrays the exclusive standards of the élite group to which he has been admitted. *Satires* II is markedly different.[42] In this book Horace takes a back seat – or even leaves the stage altogether – and introduces a variety of new characters, wise men and fools who have a message to deliver. Whereas Book I consisted of monologues (even I.9 is a monologue: a narrative reporting a dialogue), six of the eight poems of Book II are dialogues, dialogues, moreover, in which Horace generally takes the minor role. Horace is not here a directive or authoritative figure but a passive character who may even become the victim of his more talkative and assertive interlocutor. This leaves more work for the reader to do in deciding how to react to the chief character. In this respect, the label 'the Roman Socrates' may be applied most rewardingly to Horace's *persona* in Book II,[43] as a reference to Plato's portrayal of Socrates in which he allows his interlocutors to pursue their ideas and theories until they reveal their folly or impossibility.[44] In Book II, then, Horace presents a homogenous, consistent, static *persona*. And in place of the 'story-line' of Book I, the patterning and balance between poems is more evident in Book II, as has long been recognized.[45]

The book opens with a consultation poem, in which Horace seeks advice from Trebatius, an eminent lawyer, about whether he should continue to write satire.[46] This is the third poem (after I.4 and I.10) in which Horace appeals to Lucilius as a precedent[47] and the evidence strongly suggests that this poem, or at least its ending, is closely modelled upon Lucilius' programmatic poem in which he defends his choice of satire.[48] It is interesting to note that Horace's earlier criticisms of Lucilius have disappeared and that he now finds it most useful to evoke the autobiographical mode established by Lucilius (30–4)[49] and his intimacy with the powerful of his day, namely Scipio Aemilianus and coterie (71–4). These two features virtually epitomize the character which emerged at the end of *Satires* I. The playfulness in this poem, amounting 'almost to farce'[50] and culminating with a note of humour in the pun on *carmina bona* and *carmina mala*,[51] is typical of the more self-assured *persona*, immune from envious attack (lines 74–8), presented in *Satires* II.

The balancing consultation is II.5, the only poem in the book in which 'Horace' does not feature. The poem is a humorous version of Odysseus' meeting with the prophet Tiresias in *Odyssey* 11.[52] In this epic parody, Ulysses asks a final question of the prophet: 'Can you suggest ways and means of recovering the property I've lost?' (2–3) He receives in reply a disquisition upon the thoroughly Roman topic of legacy-hunting. Tiresias' advice bears no relation to morality but is based entirely upon expediency. The debunking of Homer's characters by their portrayal as cynical and mercenary makes the poem high in entertainment value but low on advice, rather as *Sat.* II.1 was.

A second pair of poems in Book II are the Stoic sermons, II.3 and II.7. These poems clearly indicate the distance Horace's *persona* has travelled from Book I, because here Horace is the captive audience of philosophical diatribes of the kind which his *persona* delivered in the first three poems of Book I. Both poems contain a Stoic lecture set within a conversation which serves to introduce the main speaker, Damasippus in II.3[53] and Davus in II.7.[54] Both protagonists are simply repeating lectures heard or told to them and both present extreme Stoic paradoxes, Damasippus that only the wise man is sane and Davus that only the wise man is free. Both are humorous because of the incompatibility between the man and the message: Damasippus the dealer and entrepreneur, obsessed with making money but now bankrupt, presumes to harangue Horace at such length on sanity; and Davus the slave reiterates a lecture on freedom to his master. The Saturnalian setting of both poems is an important clue to their frivolity, likewise the humorous endings in which Horace loses his patience and his temper.

The even-numbered poems in Book II all take food and feasts as their subject-matter. This not only reflects the centrality of the dinner (*cena*) as a social occasion in Roman society but follows a precedent established by Lucilius, whose *Satires* included several feasts, possibly inspired by Ennius' *Hedyphagetica* ('Delicatessen').[55]

Food is used in II.2 and II.6, the two monologues in the book, as a gauge of life. In II.2 Horace reports the words of wisdom of the country-dweller Ofellus, whom he labels 'an unprofessional philosopher of sturdy common sense' (line 3), thus inviting us to accept his views. Ofellus advocates moderation in food: the avoidance of luxury on the one hand and also of stinginess on the other. This amounts to a recommendation of self-sufficiency and independence (e.g. 126–7: 'Whatever new horrors and upheavals Fortune brings she can't take much away from that'), themes of wider significance that will feature more prominently later in Horace's satirical works. *Satires* II.6 explores the same themes, again with particular reference to food, in the Aesop fable of the City Mouse and the Country Mouse with which the poem ends.[56] The poem centres upon a contrast between life in the city and life in the country.[57] We are invited to value the country as a place of relaxation and retreat from the duties, hassles, and competition of city life. Particularly evocative is Horace's description of the meals with friends he enjoys in the country (65–76). Just such a meal is the setting for the telling of the fable which also values the safety and independence of country life over the luxury and danger of city life. Despite this idealization of the country, we should not forget that his connection with Maecenas is 'sweet music' in Horace's ears (32), and that his celebration of country life is an indirect expression of thanks to Maecenas for his gift of the Sabine farm.[58]

Food appears in the pair of poems, II.4 and II.8, as a vehicle of criticism. In II.4 Horace persuades Catius to repeat to him the lecture about food which he has just heard, rather as Damasippus (II.3) and Davus (II.7) repeat their Stoic sermons. Catius reveals himself as a fool and an obsessive in his elevation of the topic of food to the level of philosophy.[59] Horace indicates his disdain and sense of superiority indirectly in the ironic tone of his remarks to Catius in the conversation which frames the lecture. In II.8 Fundanius, a comic dramatist and member of Maecenas' entourage, narrates to Horace the events of the dinner-party which he attended with Maecenas and others the previous day. The narration mocks the host, Nasidienus, as a pretentious and ostentatious man who continually offends

Maecenas in his attempts to impress him.[60] The theme of this poem is taken up several decades later by Petronius in his 'Feast of Trimalchio', (*Cena Trimalchionis*, part of his *Satyrica*) which likewise, but in much greater detail, satirizes the vulgar ostentation of a *nouveau riche*. The poem, the last in Book II, has a similar function to I.10: its ending emphasizes the exclusivity of Maecenas' clique and the impossibility of people like Nasidienus ever comprehending the requisite standards of conduct.

In his second book of *Satires*, then, Horace presents a *persona* confident in his position as a member of Maecenas' circle who continues to uphold the standards of decorum of that circle. He adopts a Socratic position in relation to the numerous interlocutors he allows on to the stage and invites the audience to share his superior view of them. This is a more subtle and demanding type of satire than Book I, which was more direct, and it paves the way for further subtlety and indirectness in his later satirical works.

Epistles

Both Horace's own testimony and other ancient evidence indicates that his *Epistles* are a continuation of the *Satires*, or, to put it another way, that Horace's *Satires* and his *Epistles* were simply two different forms of the genre *satura*, Roman hexameter satire.[61] The fact that Lucilius used the letter form in several of his *Satires* (e.g. 186–9 W = 181–8 M and possibly 689–719 W) and that he refers to the *epistula* as an example of a small verse form (404 W =341 M) adds weight to this view.[62] But the overwhelming evidence is provided by the poems themselves. In form, content, tone, and treatment they closely resemble the *Satires*.[63]

Epistles I is a carefully constructed collection of twenty poems of varying lengths, addressees, and themes.[64] Several emphasize the poetic fiction that these are 'real' letters[65] by asking for or offering snippets of personal or national news (I.3, I.4, I.8, I.10, I.11, I.12, I.15) or by resemblance to a particular type of letter (I.5, an invitation to dinner; I.9 and I.12, letters of recommendation) or even by inclusion of epistolary formulae (I.6 closes with 'Good-bye and good luck.').

Most continue the themes of the *Satires*, in the form of Horace offering advice on how to live, on matters of education and literature. No single philosophy is advocated in *Epistles* I, nor should we expect one if we accept Horace's programmatic statement of inconsistency early in the opening poem, dedicated to Maecenas (I.1.14–19):

> I don't feel bound to swear obedience to any master.
> Where the storm drives me I put ashore and look for shelter.

> Now I'm a man of action and plunge into civic affairs,
> doing my highest duty with stern and selfless devotion;
> now I slip quietly back to the rules of Aristippus, attempting
> to induce things to conform to me, not vice versa.

Instead, he tailors his advice to his addressees, selecting material from different Hellenistic philosophies. Thus the Epicurean concept of living for the day appears in I.4 and I.5 and the Pythagorean motto 'never be dazzled' in I.6. *Epistles* I.1 and I.16 criticize the extreme manifestation of Stoicism and in I.17 Aristippus' versatility is valued above the rigid asceticism (*asperitas*) of the Cynic Diogenes.

But the chief positive ideals which emerge belong to no single philosophical school: these are tolerance, tranquillity, and independence.[66] Throughout the book, he exhibits tolerance towards his addressees, by not prescribing their behaviour but simply offering advice, often with a touch of self-irony. The most memorable example of this is probably the close of I.4 where he describes himself as 'a porker from Epicurus' herd'. Tranquillity is frequently connected with withdrawal to the country (I.4, I.7, I.10, I.14) although in I.11 Horace asserts that his ideal of a 'balanced mind' (*aequus animus*) is available anywhere.[67] Independence is a theme of central importance. In I.19, addressed to his patron Maecenas, Horace asserts his literary independence. More significantly, perhaps, in I.7, also addressed to Maecenas, Horace explores his relationship with his patron by expressing his own desire for independence and by encouraging Maecenas towards tolerance. As in the *Satires*, Horace presents a flattering picture of the relationship, while making the point that concerns him, e.g. *Epistles* I.7.37–9:

> You have often praised my modesty; I've called you 'Father' and 'Sir'
> in your hearing; nor do I use less generous terms in your absence.
> If you try me, you'll find I can cheerfully hand your presents back.

The themes of relations between the powerful and their dependents is taken up again in the last two substantial poems in the book, I.17 and I.18.[68] The first, addressed to an unknown 'Gauche' (Scaeva), evidently a poor dependent, contains humorous advice on not being too demanding of one's patron. The second is addressed to Lollius, the young man to whom Horace offers advice on the educational value of poetry in I.2. Here he recommends a middle course in relations with a patron between being a sponger and being rude. Loyalty, integrity, and tolerance are the qualities required in friendship with the great. The final lines of the poem round off the book (I.19 is a literary manifesto and I.20, addressed as a joke to the book, is a humorous sketch of the author) with a quintessential blending of themes (I.18.107–12):

> May I have what I have now, or less, and live for myself
> what's left of my life (if heaven decides that *any* is left);
> may I have a decent supply of books and enough food
> for the year; may my spirits not depend on the hour's caprice.
> And yet it's enough to ask Jove, the giver and taker,
> to grant me life and subsistence; I'll find my own stability.

Significantly, Horace ends with an assertion of self-sufficiency: he will provide his own 'stability', *aequus animus*.

Both in terms of themes – friendship, morality, education, independence – and techniques – the self-ironic autobiographical presentation incorporating anecdotes, fables, proverbs, and literary references and allusions – *Epistles* I closely resembles the earlier *Satires*. Moreover, the *persona* presented in *Epistles* I is a natural development from *Satires* I and II. In *Satires* I Horace initially adopted the role of teacher and preacher to the masses, then cast himself as advocate and defender of the standards of Maecenas' set. In *Satires* II, he maintained this stance with a less obtrusive *persona*, taking the back seat while various interlocutors revealed their folly. In *Epistles* I Horace's *persona* is similarly indirect, as he offers varied advice to a variety of addressees, mostly friends and mostly younger men. The form of the book allows him to explore different ways of living: the collection is a reflection of the variety and complexity of life.

Epistles II broadly continues this stance but with a shift towards a more teacherly pose by Horace, chiefly because the poems are significantly longer. Moreover, it cannot be irrelevant that Horace attained unquestionably supreme status as a poet at this point in his career, in that Augustus commissioned him to write the *Secular Hymn* (*carmen saeculare*) for the Secular Games in 17 B.C. In view of this, it is not surprising to find Horace offering advice especially on literary matters in *Epistles* II.[69]

Epistles II consists of *Epistles* II.1,[70] addressed to Augustus himself, and *Epistles* II.2,[71] addressed to Florus, a young man of Tiberius' circle of friends. There is considerable debate whether or not the so-called *Ars poetica*[72] also belongs in *Epistles* II. My view is that it does indeed belong here, partly because the combined length of the three *Epistles* is just that of an Augustan poetry book, but chiefly because it shares the themes and techniques of the rest of Horace's writings in the genre *satura*. If this is accepted, it is more properly referred to as *Epistles* II.3.[73] This poem too is presented as a letter, addressed to the Piso family who were evidently poets or aspiring poets themselves.

The three poems feature themes familiar from *Satires* I and II and *Epistles* I: morality, education, literature and philosophy, friendship and right conduct. Moreover they continue the earlier conversational tone and unelevated flavour, incorporating illustrations from many varied activities together with the autobiographical mode of presentation including a strong element of self-irony.

In *Epistles* II.1 and II.3 Horace focusses his discussion of poetry around the 'public' genres, namely epic and drama; in *Epistles* II.2 the same issue arises in his refusal to write lyric poetry in favour of more serious moral and philosophical concerns. In all three Horace attaches great importance to standards: both in conduct and in literature correct behaviour (*decorum*) is necessary. All three poems have an informal, highly selective presentation with no obvious systematization. It would be difficult to use any of them as a handbook or a textbook and this alone is perhaps the most telling argument against regarding *Epistles* II.3 as an *ars*, with all the accompanying implications of rigour and system. Significant support for this view lies in the humorous light-weight close of all three poems, of which the most memorable is the picture of the mad poet, compared with a bear and then a leech, with which *Epistles* II.3 closes.

In all these respects and more, *Epistles* II resembles Horace's earlier poems in the genre of *satura*.[74] The *persona* in *Epistles* II also continues the (ironically) modest presentation with which we are familiar, here particularly in his disclaimers of poetic ability. What is different is Horace's overt adoption of the role of teacher in all three poems (e.g. *Epistles* II.3.306–8) and his consequent use of a more didactic tone in places. In this respect, *Epistles* II represents a further development from *Epistles* I. At first sight it may appear that Horace's satiric *persona* has come full circle – that is, he has reverted to the role of teacher/preacher which we met in the opening poems of *Satires* I. But Horace has in fact travelled up a spiral. He does indeed adopt the role of teacher in *Epistles* II, but from the position not of an outsider (as in *Satires* I.1–3) but of an insider. His upward social mobility has given him a position of authority and expertise from which he can pronounce on literary and moral matters. Horace takes on this role in order to state still more definitively than before the standards set by the powerful group with which he is associated. Horace's second book of *Epistles* is a celebration of the Augustan ideal.

NOTES

1. Armstrong (1986).
2. On Horace and Maecenas see Rudd (1986), pp. 51–62, Armstrong (1970), 91–102.
3. The best text of Horace is that of F.Klingner (5th edition, Leipzig, 1970). There are many studies of Horace. Reckford (1969) and Armstrong (1989) provide a sound orientation, Williams (1972) provides an overview with copious bibliography; and Fraenkel (1957) provides a wealth of scholarship and detailed interpretation. West (1967) offers acute literary criticism of a few poems; Costa (1973) contains a collection of essays of varying quality; Shackleton Bailey (1982) presents his view of the man and his poetry. For a full bibliography see Kissel (1981).
4. Views on the date of *Epistles* II.1 range from soon after 17 B.C. (Williams (1972), p. 39) to 12 B.C. (Rudd (1989), pp. 1–2); and range even wider on the date of the *Ars Poetica*, from the period 23–17 B.C. (Williams (1972), pp. 38–9) to the 'blank' period in Horace's output, 13–8 B.C. (e.g. Rudd (1989), pp. 19–21). After a full examination of the evidence, Brink (1963), pp. 239–43 concludes that it is not possible to date the *Ars poetica*. See now Frischer (1991), pp. 48–9: date 24–20 B.C.
5. Bion represents Hellenistic diatribe, an important influence upon Horace: see above page 18 and note 9. The title of what we usually call the *Satires* is problematical. It is likely that we should refer to these poems as *Sermones* rather than *Satires* and that the term *satura* designates the genre. For a review of the ancient testimony, including that in Horace, see Rudd (1966), pp. 154–9. On the question of the genre of the *Epistles* see below notes 61–3.
6. All the general books on Roman satire devote substantial sections to Horace and provide a useful introduction to the poems in the *Satires* (only Knoche includes the *Epistles*): Anderson (1982), pp. 13–49 (= Sullivan (1963), pp. 1–37), Witke (1970), pp. 49–78, Ramage, Sigsbee & Fredericks (1974), pp. 64–88, Knoche (1975), pp. 73–98, Coffey (1989), pp. 63–97. More specialized discussions of Horace's satirical works appear in the notes below; for a full discussion of every poem in *Satires* I and II Rudd (1966) must be the first resort. Editions of Horace's satirical works include E. C. Wickham (Oxford, 1891), A. Palmer[4] (London, 1891: *Satires*), A. S. Wilkins (London, 1896: *Epistles*), P. Lejay (Paris, 1911: *Satires*), Kiessling-Heinze[6] (Berlin, 1957), Brink (1971) and (1982) (*Epistles* II and *Ars poetica*), Rudd (1989) (*Epistles* II and *Ars poetica*). The best translation of Horace's satirical works is that of Rudd (1987).
7. For a general overview of the poems in *Satires* I see: Ramage, Sigsbee & Fredericks (1974), pp. 65–76; Coffey (1989), pp. 70–81; Anderson (1982), pp. 28–41; Armstrong (1989), pp. 26–48; Williams (1972), pp. 15–20 (on *Satires* I and II). Fiske (1920), pp. 219–368 combines careful analysis of the poems of *Satires* I with indications of the influence of Lucilius upon Horace. Rudd (1966) contains analysis of the poems as follows: 'The Diatribes of Book I' (I.1, I.2, I.3), pp. 1–35; 'Poet and Patron' (I.6), pp. 36–53; 'Entertainments' (I.5, I.7, I.8, I.9), pp. 54–85; 'Horace and Lucilius' (I.4, I.10, II.1) 86–131.
8. Cf. Zetzel (1980), pp. 60–2, Anderson (1982), pp. 28–9.
9. Zetzel (1980), esp. pp. 63–4.
10. On diatribe in Horace, see Coffey (1989), pp. 92–3, Morford (1984), pp. 15–17 and more generally OCD^2 Diatribe', Oltramare (1924).
11. The philosophical flavour can best be described as non-doctrinaire Epicureanism, in accord with Maecenas' own tendency: DuQuesnay (1984), p. 33.
12. See Bushala (1971) on the theme of the poem, Curran (1970) on the use of obscenity and Richlin (1983), pp. 174–7 on Lucilian and Horatian concerns in the poem.
13. Ennius *Ann.* 471–2 W = 465–6 V[3].
14. McKeown (1979), 73.
15. As Henderson's reading of the poem (1989a), pp. 104–8 suggests in its explication of the crude fetishization of women. Cf. Bushala (1971).
16. Rudd's title (1966), pp. 1–35. On these three poems as a triad see Armstrong (1964).
17. See DuQuesnay (1984), pp. 35–6.
18. On lines 63–5 see Shackleton Bailey (1982), pp. 24–5.
19. On the literary principles expressed in this poem, see Brink (1963), pp. 156–64.
20. We should beware of reading this as autobiography and, as in I.6, should focus upon the literary value of Horace's father: Anderson (1982), pp. ix-x, Leach (1971).
21. Cf. Dickie (1981), pp. 185–93: 'it is the moral framework of friendship and its duties within

which Horace defends his writing satire'; see Hunter (1985), 486-90, Muecke (1979), LaFleur (1981), 1794-1801; on the importance of frankness throughout Horace's poetry see DeWitt (1935); on the flexibility of the concept of *libertas* see Rudd (1957).

22. Fiske (1920), pp. 306-16.
23. Thus Classen (1973).
24. On the political backdrop DuQuesnay (1984), pp. 39-43.
25. The whole of the poem praises Maecenas either directly or subtly: DuQuesnay (1984), pp. 43-52. On Horace's exaggeration of his poverty see Armstrong (1986).
26. Thus e.g. Armstrong (1989), p. 41.
27. On the political significance of I.7 and Horace's subtlety of treatment see DuQuesnay (1984), pp. 36-8.
28. Anderson (1982), p. 80, referring to Buchheit (1968), pp. 542-6 (which is summarized by van Rooy (1971), 70-1); on *Sat.* I.7 as a reworking of a satire by Lucilius see van Rooy (1971), 87-90.
29. See Anderson's excellent discussion of the poem (1982), pp. 74-83 and DuQuesnay (1984), pp. 38-9 on the possible political dimension.
30. A less complimentary view of Priapus and the masculine aggression which he epitomizes is forcefully put by Hallett (1981) and Henderson (1989a), pp. 108-12; the debate centres upon whether or not the fart is involuntary or deliberate.
31. Anderson (1982), pp. 82-3.
32. Line 78. The allusion is to Hom. *Il.* 20.443, which is quoted by Lucilius 267 W (= 231 M), a fact which Fiske (1920), pp. 330-6 uses to argue for a Lucilian original to Horace's poem. On the significance of the allusion see Fraenkel (1957), p. 118.
33. Anderson (1982), pp. 84-102.
34. Humour is present too in Horace's use of law: see Cloud (1989), pp. 65-7.
35. Brink (1963), pp. 165-71. On the shift from I.4 see LaFleur (1981), 1803-8. On the elements of Callimacheanism here see Scodel (1987).
36. DuQuesnay (1984), pp. 27-32.
37. DuQuesnay (1984), esp. pp. 56-8.
38. Shackleton Bailey (1982), p. 64 rightly labels him 'an inveterate snob'.
39. Cf. van Rooy (1973), who overstates some of the echoes.
40. Zetzel's phrase. On the question of the title of these poems see above note 5.
41. E.g. the series of detailed studies of the poems by van Rooy (1968), (1970a), (1970b), (1971), (1972a), (1972b).
42. For a general overview of the poems in *Satires* II see: Williams (1972), pp. 15-20; Ramage, Sigsbee & Fredericks (1974), pp. 76-84; Coffey (1989), pp. 81-90; Armstrong (1989), pp. 48-55. Anderson (1982), pp. 41-9 provides an important analysis. Fiske (1920), pp. 369-424 discusses the literary background with special reference to Lucilius. Rudd (1966), pp. 86-131 examines II.1 in conjunction with I.4 and I.10; 'The Diatribes of Book II' (II.2, II.3, II.7), pp. 160-201; 'Food and Drink' (II.4 and II.8), pp. 202-23; 'A Consultation' (II.5), pp. 224-42; 'Poet and Patron' (II.6), pp. 243-57.
43. Anderson (1982), pp. 41-9 helpfully contrasts the *personae* adopted in Books I and II by comparing them with the portrayals of Socrates by Xenophon and Plato respectively. It is a little misleading that he labels the *persona* of Book I 'The Socratic Moralist' ((1982), p. 28) when this label evidently applies to both books.
44. On Horace's debt in *Satires* II to Plato in his use of dialogue and character see Fraenkel (1957), pp. 136-7 and Haight (1947).
45. See Boll (1913), Port (1926), pp. 288-91, Ludwig (1968).
46. Actually a parody of a legal consultation: Cloud (1989), p. 67.
47. On the development of Horace's handling of literary and legal matters in I.4, I.10 and II.1 see Brink (1963), pp. 153-77, LaFleur (1981), esp. 1812-26.
48. For the literature on the 'pattern of apology' see LaFleur (1981), 1811 n. 58, esp. Shero (1922), Kenney (1962) and Griffith (1970).
49. On the use of autobiography see the excellent article of Harrison (1987).
50. Rudd (1966), p. 129.
51. See Griffith (1970), 60-1, Coffey (1989), p. 82 with 231 n.83, Cloud (1989) p. 67, Clauss (1985), 205, who indicates the Callimachean elements, including humour, in the poem.
52. See Roberts (1984).
53. See Bond (1987).

54. See Bond (1978).
55. On the *cena* in Roman Satire see Shero (1923). According to Fiske (1920), p. 420 Lucilius included satires on banquets in Books 4, 5, 13, 20, and 21.
56. See West (1974) for a model example of literary criticism of the fable. Also Witke (1970), pp. 61–76 on the poem as a whole.
57. See Braund (1989), pp. 39–43.
58. On Horace's relationship with Maecenas and treatment of him as a god in this poem see Bond (1985).
59. Hudson (1989), pp. 80–1. This is particularly entertaining if we accept Classen's identification of Catius as a (misguided) follower of Epicurus: Classen (1978).
60. Hudson (1989), pp. 83–5. On the superiority shown by the narrator here, reminiscent of I.5, see McGann (1973), pp. 66–7.
61. At *Ep*. II.2.59–60, II.1.4 and II.1.251 Horace seems to include the *Epistles* in the designation *sermones*. Quintilian, writing towards the end of the first century A.D., refers to Horace as a writer of lyric (*I.O.* 1.8.6), iambic (*I.O.* 10.1.96) and satirical (*I.O.* 10.1.94) poetry and makes no separate mention of the *Epistles*. Suetonius bears out the generic identification in his biography of Horace, written early in the second century A.D., when he adduces passages from the *Epistles* and locates them 'in his satires'. The scholiast Porphyrio (third century) regards the *Satires* and the *Epistles* as belonging to the genre *satura* and differing in title (*Sermones, Epistulae*), the one addressed to someone present and other to someone absent. Pseudo-Acro's comment (no earlier than the fifth century A.D.) on *Ep*. I.1 indicates that the only difference is the presence or absence of addressees: 'for in letters we speak to those absent, in conversation to those present'(*epistulis enim ad absentes loquimur, sermone cum praesentibus*); similar is Demetrius' remark that 'a letter is one half of a conversation' (233 = III p. 311 Sp.). The title of the *Epistles* was recently debated in the pages of *Liverpool Classical Monthly* 4 (1979).
62. Fiske (1920), pp. 425–75 offers telling evidence in the form of the influence of Lucilius upon Horace's *Epistles*, including the *Ars poetica*.
63. On the *Epistles* as a continuation of the *Satires* see Hendrickson (1897), Williams (1972), p. 36, Rudd (1989), pp. 11–12; for a review of the evidence see Rudd (1966), pp. 154–9; Kilpatrick (1986), p. xiv rightly observes that 'there is as great a difference between *Satires* I and II as between *Satires* II and the *Epistles*'. For an overview of the *Epistles* see Williams (1972), pp. 36–41 (*Epistles* I and II); for a brief orientation Knoche (1975), pp. 89–92, Anderson (1982), pp. 68–73, Armstrong (1989), pp. 117–35 on *Epistles* I and 153–62 on *Epistles* II.
64. Fraenkel deems this 'the most harmonious of Horace's books' ((1957) p. 309). We are fortunate to have two good, recent studies of *Epistles* I, McGann (1969), who focusses upon the philosophical background and literary texture of the poems (see especially his poem-by-poem analysis in Chapter 2, 'The Texture of Argument', pp. 33–87), and Kilpatrick (1986), who provides an excellent brief introduction to the book (pp. xiii-xxiv) followed by detailed analysis of the twenty poems with useful bibliography, pp. 157–70 including poem-by-poem bibliography. See also Reckford (1969), pp. 107–118 who highlights the central themes of the book, Dilke (1973) and Williams (1968), pp. 1–30 who clears the ground for literary appreciation of *Epistles* I.
65. On this question see Williams (1968), pp. 7–24, McGann (1969), pp. 89–100 and Kilpatrick (1986), p. xvii who urges that 'they are best judged as fictional discourse'.
66. On the philosophical content of *Epistles* I see McGann (1969), pp. 9–32 and Moles (1985); on the ethical concerns in the book see Macleod (1979); Mayer (1986) and (1985) urges that appropriate conduct or 'good manners' and not philosophy is the chief concern of *Epistles* I.
67. The antithesis between country and city and the connection between this and other themes in the *Epistles* is emphasized by Hirth (1985).
68. On clients and patrons in Horace *Epistles* I (7, 17, 18) see Morford (1977), 226–9.
69. I have not seen Kilpatrick (1989) on *Epistles* II.
70. On which see Reckford (1969), pp. 138–45, Fraenkel (1957), pp. 383–99, Rudd (1989), pp. 1–11 for introduction and 75–122 for commentary, Brink (1982), pp. 31–265 for detailed commentary and 464–95 for analysis.
71. On which see Reckford (1969), pp. 119–22, Rudd (1989), pp. 12–19 for introduction and 122–50 for commentary, Brink (1963), pp. 183–90, (1982), pp. 266–412 for detailed commentary and 496–522 for analysis, McGann (1954) and Rutherford (1981) for interpretation.
72. On which see Reckford (1969), pp. 138–45; Rudd (1989), pp. 19–37 for introduction and 150–229 for commentary; Brink (1963), pp. viii-ix, 153–6, 213–38 on the *Ars* as literary criticism and

(1971), pp. 445–523 for an analysis of the poem 'as Horatian poetry'; and Brink (1971), pp. 73–431 for commentary containing a wealth of useful material.

73. In the manuscript tradition the *Ars poetica* is associated with the lyric poems not the satires; and Quintilian in the first century A.D. (a good deal earlier than the earliest extant manuscript) refers to the poem as *ars poetica* (*I.O.*, Preface to Trypho 2) and at *I.O.* 8.3.60 as the *liber de arte poetica*. However, a fourth-century grammariam Charisius cites a passage from the poem as 'Horatius in Epistularum' and there are strong grounds for calling the poem the *Epistula ad Pisones* (thus Rudd (1989), p. 19). On the *Ars poetica* as *Epistles* II.3 see Williams (1972), pp. 38–41, Armstrong (1989), p. 154.

74. For example the influence of Lucilius persists: Fiske (1913), pp. 1–16 and 34–5 demonstrates the influence of Lucilius upon the so-called *Ars poetica*.

V. PERSIUS

The next satirist whose work survives is Persius, whose brief book of *Satires* was acclaimed during his lifetime and after his death.[1] Aulus Persius Flaccus, A.D. 34–62, was born at Volaterrae in Etruria into an important family of equestrian status. He was educated at Rome as a pupil of Cornutus, a Stoic who was a freedman of Seneca, and was associated with the group of Stoic politicians which wielded considerable power at Rome, including the senator Thrasea Paetus whose wife, Arria, was a relative of Persius and who wrote a biography of the Stoic hero Cato the Younger. Persius evidently did not participate in politics but seems to have moved in high circles, given his acquaintance with the poet Lucan, five years younger.[2]

In his short life, he wrote only one book of *Satires*, consisting of six poems preceded by a prologue in limping iambics.[3] The Book may or may not be complete and was not published until after his death; whichever the case, it is clear that his poems were written for an audience which shared Persius' own high level of education, because they are packed with literary echoes and allusions. In particular, he shows an intimate familiarity with the satirical works of Lucilius and Horace.[5] Yet, despite this, his *Satires* are entirely original. He has taken the genre and adapted it to produce a type of satire which is not only distinctive but highly significant in the development of the genre. He is responsible for creating the character of the angry and alienated young man.[6]

He presents a stance of scornful isolation immediately, in the prologue, in which he describes himself as 'a semi-clansman' (*semipaganus*, line 6, a word coined by Persius for this occasion), that is, not a full member of the group of bards: he rejects their poetic imagery of inspiration and asserts that money is their inspiration. Even his choice of a non-hexameter metre for the prologue marks out his rebellion: he uses the choliambic metre as a signal of his more aggressive stance.[7] This stance is confirmed in the opening lines of the first satire where he appears to be quite content with a small or non-existent audience (1.1–3):

> *O men's anxieties! O the emptiness in things!*
> 'Who'll read that?' Asking me? Good heavens, no one. 'No one?'
> P'raps two, p'raps no one.

He is more explicit about his preferred audience at the end of this poem: the devotee of Greek Old Comedy, who approves of 'concentrates' (125), not the silly and superficial person who mocks education and philosophy. And throughout this poem – a programmatic statement of his genre – he confirms this isolationist stance by a wholesale rejection of contemporary poetry on the grounds that it is too smooth, weak, and artificial. He uses striking imagery to justify his rejection of modern literature and his choice of satire. The low standard of modern literature is portrayed in moral terms drawn in particular from homosexuality and effeminacy and disease, discussed in detail by Bramble.[8] Satire, by contrast, is characterized as excrement and then as direct and indirect attack (1.112–118):

> 'Public nuisance here forbidden' you say.
> Paint up two snakes. *Boys, This Ground's Holy. Piss Elsewhere.*
> I'm moving on. Lucilius carved up the town –
> *You, Lupus, Mucius, you* – and broke his back teeth on them.
> Sly Flaccus for his laughing friend touches each fault
> And, once admitted, round the heart plays mocking games,
> Skilful to hang the public from that sniffy nose.

In this way Persius not only states his chosen genre – he will follow in the footsteps of Lucilius and Horace – but also establishes immediately his chosen *persona* of the angry, uncompromising, and rebellious young man asserting his independence with no desire to please contemporary tastes.

The rejection of society and its standards is maintained throughout the book. Frequently his ideal of independence and self-reliance is expressed in the uncompromising terms of extreme Stoicism, which is his 'idiom'.[9] The intolerance of contemporary morality and literature expressed in *Satire* 1 is followed by an intolerant condemnation of the hypocrisy and foolishness of people's prayers in *Satire* 2, a poem which ends on a 'holier-than-thou' note which contrasts strongly with the self-ironic humility of Horace's *persona*.[10] In the third *Satire* the intolerant young student appears to have lapsed and is on the receiving end of a lecture[11] on the madness of people who will not allow philosophy to help them, a theme reminiscent of the sermon on madness in Horace *Sat.* II.3. In the extended medical imagery at the end of the poem, which imparts a strong Stoic flavour, we notice Persius' liking for using physical metaphors to convey moral and psychological matters. *Satire* 4 uses Socrates as the voice of self-knowledge in conversation with the young politician Alcibiades whose superficiality and lack of knowledge and expertise is attacked.[12] The two anecdotes follow which illustrate how 'We snipe at others' legs and expose our own to arrows' (42).

All this is ammunition towards the central message of the poem, 'Spit out what isn't you' (51), which is Persius' typically physical and graphic version of the ancient Delphic maxim 'Know thyself'.

Satire 5, the longest in the Book, draws together many of the themes and characteristics of Persius' satire. The poem begins in a strongly autobiographical mode as a personal tribute to Cornutus, Persius' instructor in Stoicism (lines 21–2):

> We speak in private. At Camena's instance now
> I give my heart for your inspection.

Whatever the reality of the relationship between Persius and Cornutus, there can be no doubt that in *Satire* 5 it is closely modelled upon Horace's presentation of his relationship with his father in *Satires* I.4 and I.6. The poem incorporates a substantial sermon on the Stoic theme of freedom, a theme treated in Horace *Satires* II.7. Where Horace distanced himself from the 'message' there by having his slave Davus re-tell the sermon reported to him by the porter who had overheard it and by portraying his own intolerance of the 'message', here Persius presents a fully-fledged performance by a Stoic extremist[13] and in effect leaves us to draw our own conclusions about the extremism and offensiveness of the views expressed. The only corrective occurs in the final lines, with the picture of varicose soldiers mocking the sentiments of the sermon.

The sixth *Satire* is often said to present a dramatic change in tone.[14] This view is hard to accept. The poem is presented as an epistle, following in the tradition of Lucilius and Horace.[15] But Persius' withdrawal from Rome to the Ligurian coast does not signify a shift towards contentment but rather a logical consequence and physical realization of the isolation proclaimed earlier in the book. His geographical withdrawal is a violent, symbolic expression of independence and detachment from society and its obligations: 'I'm there, unworried by the crowd . . .' (line 12). He is particularly harsh and aggressive towards his heir. He imagines his heir complaining about the diminution of his inheritance and ostentatiously resolves to indulge himself as a result. This poem, then, is a symbolic statement of Persius' independence and self-reliance and, as such, presents the essence of the aloof, detached *persona* which he adopts throughout the book.

This picture of Persius does not do justice to the dense literary texture of his poetry or to the very startling and at times humorous juxtaposition of images so well characterized in his own words, 'clever at the pointed juxtaposition' (*iunctura callidus acri* 5.14). The density of Persius' language is indicated simply by the fact that he incorporates more words per line than most classical poets.[16] This is accompanied by an unusually compressed sequence of pithy thoughts and images, most of which express abstract ideas in concrete, physical ways. A typical example of Persius' use of concrete imagery is this (3.19–24):

> Why sing
> That rigmarole? It's you to play. You're leaking madly.
> You'll be despised. When struck the pot rings false – responds
> But grudgingly, with its green clay as yet unfired.
> You're mud, both wet and soft – need turning now, and continual
> Shaping on the eager wheel.

The images of liquid flowing away, the half-baked jar, the clay on the potter's wheel all illustrate the back-sliding student who needs to study philosophy.

The closing lines of *Satire* 4 typify the collage effect of several different images in swift sequence (4.51–2):

> Spit out what isn't you; let the crowd take back what they
> have conferred; live alone, and learn how sparse your furniture is.[17]

These images are an exhortation to self-knowledge.

Persius' compressed language and startling images have a number of functions. Frequently they overturn or rejuvenate literary and philosophical clichés and commonplaces.[18] For example, the prologue and the opening of *Satire* 5 satirize the conventional language of poetic inspiration through an over-literal interpretation. The reply to (5.1–2):

> the bardic way: demand a hundred voices,
> Pray for a hundred mouths and a hundred tongues, to sing

is (5.5–6):

> Where is this leading? What great gobbets of tough song
> Do you pile up that need one hundred throats to strain?

And twice in his *Satires* he exposes the literary device of the imaginary interlocutor: at 1.44 with 'O you the anonymous whom I've just made to object' and at 6.41–2 with 'But you, my heir, whoever you are, may I have a word with you – here, in private?'

Some of Persius' images seem designed to arouse ridicule of their victims. For example, the poet with an irresistible urge to publish is given this speech (1.24–5):

> Why study, if this ferment, this wild fig-tree, once
> It has taken root, can't burst the liver and thrust through?

And 'self-indulgent Natta' is described like this (3.32–4):

> But vice has made *him* thick; prime fat has overgrown
> His nerves; he's blameless, ignorant of his loss – so deep
> Submerged he sends no further bubbles to the surface.

Such images serve to puncture pretentiousness and unveil the hypocrisy of people's behaviour and aspirations. In fact, Persius' imagery is often witty or even humorous in its perceptive debunking of figures and ideas usually treated with seriousness and respect.

Another function of Persius' imagery is to provide a source of unity to individual poems. The theme of *Satire* 1 – 'Style is the Man' – is elaborated through images drawn from disease, clothing, food and drink, homosexuality and effeminacy; similar sexual imagery equates the politician with the male prostitute in *Satire* 4. The dominant metaphor of *Satire* 3 is that of disease, spiritual and physical, while in *Satire* 5 the central theme of freedom and slavery occurs with imagery drawn from shadow and substance, food, astrology, and particularly numbers. In *Satire* 2 the theme of bribery of the gods is associated physically with food and *Satire* 6 again uses food imagery, including the banquet of life, together with the image of land and sea.[19]

Finally, the imagery is an important element of Persius' rejection of society: he presents startling, shocking metaphors which contrast starkly with the smoothness of contemporary poetry. For example (1.104–6):

> This spineless stuff is lip-deep –
> Saliva-flotsam – and the Maenad's wet, like this –
> Never bangs the desk or tastes of bitten nails.

His graphic language deglamourizes and hence it is a central element of his satire – and undoubtedly his most important and original contribution to the genre.

NOTES

1. During his lifetime: 'But Lucanus so admired Flaccus's writings that he hardly restrained himself while reciting from a shout that Flaccus's were real poems but he himself was merely playing about' (*Life of Persius* 5 = lines 21–4); after his death: Quintilian *I.O.* 10.1.94: 'Persius has won a high and justified reputation, although he wrote only one book'.
2. For more detail about Persius' circumstances and acquaintances see Morford (1984), pp. 1–12.
3. The best text of Persius is that of Clausen (Oxford (1956), Oxford Classical Text (with Juvenal) (1966)). Recent years have seen the production of several new translations and commentaries which supplement that of Conington (1874): Jenkinson (1980) includes text, introduction, an acute prose

translation and fairly brief commentary; Harvey (1981), which includes neither text nor translation, is thorough and detailed; Merwin's (1981) verse translation is unauthentically accessible and does not convey the force of Persius' language; Rudd (1987); Lee & Barr (1987) combines a new verse translation by Lee with brief introduction and generally helpful commentary by Barr. The translations used here are those of Lee and (less frequently) Rudd.

The books on Roman satire offer an introduction to Persius and his poems: Nisbet (1963); Ramage, Sigsbee & Fredericks (1974), pp. 114–35 (an excellent appreciation of the poems and their characteristics); Knoche (1975), pp. 127–39 (brief and not entirely favourable); Coffey (1989), pp 98–118 (sound and helpful); Anderson's introduction to the translation of Merwin (1981), pp. 7–50; Witke (1970), pp. 79–112 (who emphasizes the Stoic features in Persius in an essay chiefly devoted to an extended analysis of *Satire* 5). See also Rudd (1982) for a brief introduction.

The studies of Persius supply more detail: Dessen (1968) emphasizes Persius' use of *personae*, imagery, and metaphor in her first chapter (pp. 1–14) and Epilogue (pp. 93–6) and in the intervening chapters she analyses helpfully the dominant metaphor in each poem; Bramble (1974) is an excellent and challenging study, but inaccessible to those without Latin; Morford (1984) provides a useful introduction and poem-by-poem overview with notes which offer sound guidance on further bibliography and his chapter on the style of Persius (pp. 73–96) is a helpful and accessible introduction to this notoriously difficult feature of Persius' poetry. Sullivan (1972) in the scope of an article gives a critique of earlier views of Persius and urges that we view him above all as a poet. For full bibliography see Squillante Saccone (1985).

4. According to his biography, the book was unfinished at the time of his death and Cornutus removed some lines from the end before he handed it over to Caesius Bassus for publication (*Life* 8 = lines 42–5), which happened soon after Persius' death and possibly as early as 63. The reliability of this tradition and precisely how much Cornutus removed must remain a matter for speculation; the book as we have it consists of 650 lines (plus the 14-line prologue), which is not necessarily too short for a poetry book (Horace's satirical Books are longer but some of Juvenal's are of comparable length).

5. Rudd's essay 'Imitation: Association of ideas in Persius' ((1976), pp. 54–83) is an astute and accessible analysis of the multitudinous reminiscences of Horace in Persius; cf. Hooley (1984). Fiske (1909) and (1913), pp. 16–36 offers ample evidence of the influence of Lucilius and Horace's so-called *Ars poetica* upon Persius.

6. Described well by Anderson (1982), pp. 169–93.

7. Iambic poetry in Greek and Latin literature was synonymous with aggression. The choliambic or scazon ('limping' iambic) was a metre invented by Hipponax (c. 540 B.C.) and taken up by the Hellenistic poet Callimachus in his iambic poetry in which he presents himself as a new Hipponax (e.g. *Iambus* 1, Dawson (1950), pp. 8–24). It is typical of Persius that he uses a Callimachean form to reject the decadent Callimacheanism of contemporary poetry: Sullivan (1985), pp. 74–114 esp. 92–100; on Persius' relationship with Callimachus see Puelma-Piwonka (1949), pp. 361–4. On the prologue generally see Waszink (1963), Rudd (1986), pp. 178–80.

8. See Bramble (1974), pp. 16–25 on the link between morality and literature; 26–59 on the types of imagery in *Satire* 1; and 67–142 for a full and uncompromising analysis of *Satire* 1. On *Satire* 1 in general see Korzeniewski (1970).

9. Against the influential view of Martin (1939) that Persius was a 'Stoic evangelist' see Reckford (1962), 490–8.

10. On *Satire* 2 as a *genethliakon*, 'birthday poem', see Brind'Amour (1971).

11. The debate about the number of speakers in this poem continues. In essence, the choice is this: (i) one character: two voices of a student; (ii) two voices: a philosopher lecturing a lazy young noble; (iii) three voices: a narrator, a student, and a critic; (iv) two voices: a narrator/student and a critic. See Lee & Barr (1987), pp. 100–1 for brief outline and references to fuller discussions, to which add Jenkinson (1973), 534–49. This issue is not confined to *Satire* 3: see Coffey (1989), p. 101 in general and e.g. Hendrickson (1928) who argues convincingly that *Satire* 1 is a monologue, not a dialogue.

12. Jenkinson's argument (1973), 521–34 that the dialogue between Socrates and Alcibiades continues beyond the opening 22 lines of the poem is very compelling.

13. Stoic features in the sermon include: the personification of Avarice and Luxury (132–53), the scene from comedy (160–74), the animal illustration (159), the appeal to 'human and natural law' (98), extremism (99) and so on: see Witke (1970), pp. 89–110 for an analysis of the poem including its Stoic features, also Martin (1939). These are highly reminiscent of Horace's Stoic sermons in *Satires* II.3 and II.7; on Persius and the diatribe see Witke (1970), pp. 110–12.

14. E.g. Dessen (1968), pp. 78–9, Ramage, Sigsbee & Fredericks (1974), p. 124, Coffey (1989), p. 111, Morford (1984), p. 65.
15. On the 'epistolary illusion' see Grimes (1972), pp. 127–32.
16. See Sullivan (1972), p. 61 and n. 11.
17. Rudd's translation captures better than Lee's the physical imagery of *respue quod non es*.
18. Cf. Bramble (1974), p. 12: 'What some critics have regarded as whimsical obscurity is an attempt to escape from the oppressive weight of convention.' See Connor (1988) on the 'stretch of the imagination' offered by Persius' *Satires*.
19. On the 'metaphorical unity' of the *Satires* see Reckford (1962), esp. 483–90; on 'dominant metaphors' see Dessen (1968) and on sexual imagery see Richlin (1983), pp. 185–90; on the imagery in *Satire* 1 see Bramble (1974), pp. 26–59; in *Satire* 2 Flintoff (1982); in *Satire* 4 Reckford (1962), 484–7; in *Satire* 5 Anderson (1982), pp. 153–68; in *Satire* 6 Reckford (1962), 498.

VI. JUVENAL

Of the surviving Roman satirists, Juvenal is the one we know least about. Whereas for Horace and Persius we have ancient biographies which are of early date and seem generally reliable, the biographies of Juvenal are of later date and essentially contain only 'information' drawn from the *Satires*. Failure to appreciate Juvenal's use of a satiric *persona* renders these biographies worthless.

Thus there is little to be said about the life and circumstances of Decimus Iunius Iuuenalis.[1] He is the addressee of three epigrams of Martial, his younger contemporary, who calls him 'eloquent';[2] certainly the *Satires* reflect the rhetorical training received by the Roman élite.[3] The fact that his *Satires* are not dedicated to any patron may indicate that he was of relatively high social status, rather like Lucilius and Persius and in contrast with Horace. His sixteen *Satires*, of which the last breaks off in a patently unfinished state, are arranged in five books and it seems certain that they were published thus.[4] The few datable references in the *Satires* suggest that the first two books were written in the second decade of the second century A.D., either towards the end of Trajan's reign (A.D. 98–117) or, possibly, not until Hadrian's accession.[5] The third book appears to have been written early in Hadrian's reign (A.D. 117–138) and the fifth book dates from after A.D. 127.[6] It seems, then, that he was writing his *Satires* at about the same time as Tacitus was writing his Annals, which strike the modern reader as so alike in their biting tone.

Books I and II

Books I and II of Juvenal's *Satires* present an angry *persona* and are most rewardingly studied together; they may have been published together and in any case seem designed to be read as a complementary pair.[7] Book I, which contains *Satires* 1–5, handles a number of familiar themes of Roman satire with a particular emphasis on public life, the male sphere of action. In Book II, by contrast, which consists of the single enormous poem *Satire* 6, the focus is upon private life and family life, with women as the central victims of the satire. The two books together present a massive indictment of Roman life broader in scope than anything attempted by Horace or Persius.[8]

Juvenal's choice of an indignant *persona* in Books I and II may well be influenced by Persius' creation of a scathing and aloof character and, perhaps less obviously, by the maniacal fanatics brought onto the satiric stage by Horace in his second book of *Satires*. But whereas Persius' satiric *persona* prides himself upon his independence and detachment from society, Juvenal's *persona* presents himself as thoroughly immersed and involved in Roman life. This is evident in *Satire* 1, for example, when he presents himself as standing in the street and watching all the criminals and scoundrels walk by (lines 30ff., 45, 63–4). Juvenal's angry *persona* repays study because he is an interesting and complex creation. The work of Anderson on *persona* theory and its application here is of central importance.[9]

Juvenal's creation of an angry character as the mouthpiece of Book I of his *Satires* would not have presented any surprise or difficulty to his audience who had shared his experience of the Roman rhetorical education which involved a training in the adoption of different moods for different occasions. Moreover, Seneca had written treatises on anger and its opposite (*De Ira* and *De Tranquillitate Animi*) in which he offers a critique of anger. On the basis of familiarity with such ideas and possibly with these treatises, Anderson argues that Juvenal's audience was well equipped to appreciate the moral flaws in the angry man presented by Juvenal.[10]

His indignation is established rapidly by a number of stylistic features, most obviously the indignant questions, repetitions, extreme terms (e.g. 'always', 'never') and exaggerations in the very opening six lines:

> Must I be always a listener only, never hit back,
> although so often assailed by the hoarse *Theseid* of Cordus?
> Never obtain revenge when X has read me his comedies,
> Y his elegies? No revenge when my day has been wasted
> by mighty Telephus or by Orestes who, having covered
> the final margin, extends to the back, and still isn't finished?

These features occur throughout the poem, along with indications of the violence of feelings of outrage (30–1) and imagery of fire (45), to create a full characterization of an angry man. The apparent lack of structure[11] further supports this characterization.

Yet into this characterization Juvenal has also written certain contradictions which seem designed to undermine the reliability of this character. For example, he claims to be speaking reason (*rationem* 21), yet his speech is full of marks of excitement, passion, and irrationality – all the characteristics of anger just mentioned. Similarly, he strongly suggests that he is telling the truth by the device of situating himself in the street (63–4), yet his attack is full of exaggerations and generalizations, including pictures of mercenary gigolos preying on rich old women, a husband-turned-pimp, and a high-born poisoner who teaches her neighbours to murder their husbands. Again, he claims a high moral indignation (lines 30, 51–2), but shows himself envious of successful social climbers who have acquired great riches and excessively interested in sexual outrages, for example in lines 77–8, which give him away:

> Who can sleep when a daughter-in-law is seduced for money,
> when brides-to-be are corrupt, and schoolboys practise adultery?

In his claims about his chosen subject-matter too there is a discrepancy between 'theory' and 'practice'. In the famous lines 85–6 he asserts that the whole of human experience will provide him with material:

> What folks have done ever since – their hopes and fears and anger,
> their pleasures, joys, and toing and froing – is my volume's hotch-potch.

Yet within a few lines he has narrowed the focus first to vices (*uitiorum* 87) then to greed (*auaritiae* 88) as shown by his contemporaries (*quando* 87 and 88) and as illustrated by the phenomenon of the *sportula* (95–126). Lastly, his claims that he is attacking the vices of his contemporaries, rampant *now*[12] are undermined by his retreat in the final lines where, in response to a warning of the dangers he may incur by attacking people, he asserts that he will attack only the dead (170–1). These contradictions between the speaker's claims and his practice invite the audience to respond on two levels simultaneously. The first-person, quasi-autobiographical presentation encourages sympathy with the speaker's view of the world, but the discrepancies provide some distance and perspective which enable us to view the speaker as a ridiculous pessimist obsessed with money and sex.

Satire 1 is a programmatic poem. That is, it states the poet's programme or plan, containing a justification of his choice of genre ('self-defence', *apologia*, and 'refusal' of other genres, *recusatio*) together with an indication of the content, tone, and techniques.[13] In the opening lines of the poem, alternative genres including epic, drama, and elegy are rejected (1–6) as is boring mythology (7–14) in favour of the genre of Lucilius (19–21). The remainder of the poem is presented as a justification for the choice of genre based first upon a catalogue of the criminals and idiots who supposedly populate the streets of Rome (22–80) and then upon a more detailed portrayal of the particular fault of greed (81–146). This establishes not only the first-person presentation and the angry, unbalanced character of the *persona* but also the tone and content. The tone adopted is markedly different from the conversational tone of Horace and the compressed and at times obscure style of Persius. Juvenal's *persona* borrows the elevated tones of epic,[14] punctuated by lowly, mundane words, in order to indicate that satire, which uses the same metre, the dactylic hexameter, as epic, can *replace* epic because epic is remote and irrelevant whereas satire is real and immediate (e.g. 51–62). And the content is established too: the overturning of the *status quo* and the corruption and destruction of the central relationship in Roman life, that of patron and client. These are themes which have featured in earlier satire but which are confronted directly and presented pessimistically by Juvenal. In particular, Horace's interest in friendship (*amicitia*) reappears in Juvenal in the form of the relationship between patrons and clients which is at best mercenary and often broken down entirely.[15]

The final section of the poem (150–71) reiterates the choice of genre in Juvenal's reworking of what by now had evidently become a standard feature of satiric programme poems.[16] The similarities between the pattern here and that at the close of Horace *Satires* II.1 and Persius *Satire* 1 suggest that this pattern of self-defence (*apologia*) was established by Lucilius. In response to a warning by an interlocutor of the dangers of writing satire, the speaker defends his choice of genre by reference to the freedom of speech exercised by his predecessors in the genre. When the warning is repeated, the speaker then appears to give way and retreats into a humorous avoidance of the issue. Hence the declaration – patently untrue – that only the dead will be attacked.

The next poem continues the themes and tone established in *Satire* 1. In *Satire* 2 the speaker reveals a fierce hatred of homosexuals, especially passive homosexuals and effeminates, thus elaborating the theme of deviation from the 'norm' established in *Satire* 1.[17] The attack is expressed in the indignant tone with which we are already familiar, for example in lines 8–10:

> Faces are not to be trusted. Why, every street is just full
> of stern-faced sodomites. How can you lash corruption when *you*
> are the most notorious furrow among our Socratic fairies?

and supplemented by the ironic comments of the woman Laronia who is brought on stage to bolster the speaker's views in lines 36–63.[18] It begins with hypocritical moralists who try to hide their homosexuality (1–65), which is emotively called a disease (*morbum* 17), then moves to those who display their homosexuality while pronouncing upon morality (65–78).

After a graphic image of contagion spreading from the centre (79–81), the speaker switches his attack to closet (but not hypocritical) homosexuals (82–116), then to overt homosexuals (117–48). At several points in the poem occurs the idea that the corruption begins at the centre and spreads outwards (with Domitian's hypocrisy 29–33, in the image at 79–81, with the nobleman Gracchus' humiliating appearance as an effeminate type of gladiator 143–8) and this idea is emphasized at the end in the picture of young men of foreign races being corrupted into homosexuality by their visits to Rome (159–70).[19] A strand of military imagery runs through the poem as the speaker invites his audience to measure contemporary decadence against the militaristic, macho standards of the past (especially in lines 153–63).[20]

Although the speaker begins Satire 2 with a wish to flee to the edge of the world, he evidently remains in Rome. It is his friend, Umbricius, who leaves the metropolis, and his long speech explaining his departure comprises the centre-piece of the Book, *Satire* 3.[21] In the prologue the speaker sets the scene: this is a private conversation with Umbricius immediately prior to his departure in a grotto near the *porta Capena*. In the description of the grotto – it is artificial and has been taken over by Jewish beggars – and in his own criticisms of the dangers of city life, the speaker anticipates themes which Umbricius will develop in his long tirade. In effect, the prologue provides a programme for the poem, as Fredericks has shown.[22] Accordingly, Umbricius first complains that he is driven from Rome by those who are dishonest and dishonourable (21–57). Then he complains that true Romans like himself are ousted by foreigners, especially Greeks (58–125). And then he deplores the displacement of poor clients like himself by the rich (126–314). The poem finishes with a return to the conversational setting as Umbricius wishes his friend the speaker good-bye (315–22).

Throughout the poem Umbricius takes the view of the impoverished Roman client, continuing the theme of the breakdown of the patron-client relationship from *Satire* 1. He also continues the indignant tone established in *Satires* 1 and 2. A good indication of his anger is the sheer length of the tirade; a still better one is his forgetting who he is addressing when, at line 60, he bellows: 'Roman citizens, I cannot stand a Greek Rome'. In his own eyes, Umbricius is a paragon of Roman virtue, fleeing an un-Roman Rome and longing for a return of the good old days (312–14).[23] But Juvenal has him reveal that he is, rather, a jealous failure. He has tried to succeed (e.g. 91–2) but cannot compete and is, consequently, envious of those who can. That puts his departure in a different light.[24]

The speaker, though commending Umbricius' decision to leave Rome, stays behind. The next person to walk on to the stage (*ad partes* 2), so to speak, is an upstart foreigner, precisely one of the types criticized by Umbricius.[25] Crispinus in *Satire* 4 is an Egyptian who has risen to become one of the emperor Domitian's cabinet of advisers (*consilium principis*). The opening lines are an indignant attack on Crispinus for his outrageous lust and riches (1–10).[26] He is, appropriately, introduced as a 'monster of vice', *monstrum*, a strong word and a key word in the poem. At line 11 the speaker shifts to his 'lesser deeds' and tells of his self-indulgence in purchasing an expensive mullet for himself (11–27). Lines 28–33 broaden the scope of the poem by using a comparison between Crispinus and the emperor which indicates that Crispinus is small fry. The use of the archaic, epic word for emperor, *induperatorem*, at 29 perhaps provides a clue to what happens next.

The speaker pauses, takes a deep breath and intones an epic invocation of the muse, Calliope, and her sisters, the Pierides (34–6). But this is no epic poem. The comments interpolated into the invocation indicate that this is mock-epic.[27] This is proved as the narrative of the capture of an enormous turbot and its presentation to the emperor Domitian by the fisherman unfolds: epic phrases are mingled with phrases and ideas alien to epic throughout this section (37–71).[28] At 72 the epic parody turns towards the particular epic theme of the catalogue, here a catalogue of the advisers summoned to Domitian's *consilium* (72–118).[29] The final section of mock-epic narrative recounts the advice given and the dismissal of the *consilium* (119–49). In a coda to the poem, the speaker expresses the wish that Domitian had always devoted himself to such trivialities (*nugis*) instead of committing murder wantonly (150–4).

Thus the poem has a satisfying structure in which the serious crimes of Crispinus and Domitian are mentioned briefly at the beginning and end and their foolishness and frivolity is dealt with at greater length in the bulk of the poem (ABBA), in both cases in an incident involving a fish. The difference in length of treatment signifies the difference in importance between Crispinus and Domitian – and we notice, accordingly, that Crispinus as a member of Domitian's *consilium* gets a mention of only two lines (108–9). His vices and follies are a microcosm of the emperor's.[30]

The mock-epic tone of the part of the poem devoted to Domitian is new in Juvenal's first book, although not especially surprising in view of the suggestions made in *Satire* 1 that satire, because it is more relevant, replaces epic. In part, this tone is suitable simply to match the object of attack. But it seems that the epic parody has a more specific target. Statius, an epic poet writing under Domitian, wrote a poem, now lost, *On the German War* (*De Bello Germanico*), which praised Domitian's conduct of the war and included, it seems, a catalogue of the emperor's right-hand men. The three names which survive occur in Juvenal's poem.[31] Evidently the mock-epic part of the poem is a parody of parts of Statius' lost poem. This adds extra piquancy to the satire: not only are the members of the *consilium* attacked for their supine servility; so too is one of Domitian's court poets.

One of the themes of *Satire* 4 is the misuse of power and the complicity of those surrounding the source of power.[32] *Satire* 5 treats the same theme in a return to the patron-client relationship on a smaller scale than emperor-courtier. The poem presents the total breakdown of the patron-client relationship based upon mutual benefits and services, represented graphically by the two separate menus, one for the patron and his peers, the other for the lowly clients.[33] This, possibly Juvenal's finest coordination of structure and theme, satirizes the selfishness of both patron and client.

The description of the two-menu dinner is itself a vehement condemnation of the patron for failing to behave like patrons in the good old days. It is framed by passages in which the speaker criticizes the lowly client for enduring such humiliation. This is important because it highlights the shift in the speaker's sympathies in the course of Book I. In *Satire* 1, he appears to identify with the client's viewpoint; in *Satire* 3 an element of detachment is introduced in that the poor Roman client driven out of Rome is not the speaker himself but Umbricius, with whom the speaker sympathizes; and in *Satire* 5 he attacks both patrons and clients for their perversion and destruction of this central relationship.[34] This development in the character of the speaker, reminiscent perhaps of the development in Horace's satiric *persona* in *Satires* I, is a useful reminder that we are dealing with poetry and not autobiographical self-revelation.

Book I of Juvenal's *Satires* takes up themes of earlier satire, in particular the theme of friendship (*amicitia*) so important to Horace which Juvenal treats in *Satires* 1, 3, 4 and 5, with 3 as the centrepiece of the Book.[35] He combines this with the theme of food, prominent in Horace *Satires* II, particularly in *Satires* 4 and 5. The city-country dichotomy which interested Horace so much appears in *Satire* 3, although all of Book I focusses strongly on city life. What is perhaps peculiar to Juvenal is his pessimistic vision of corruption spreading from the core and tainting the whole of society. This is a particularly powerful image in *Satire* 2 but it also underlies *Satires* 3 and 4. Moreover, while exploring these themes, Juvenal has interwoven complex and subtle strands of literary texture and allusion, again following the example of his predecessors in the genre.[36] This permits his poems to be read on many levels simultaneously.

The focus in the five poems of Book I is upon public life and the foolish, selfish, and criminal acts of, primarily, men. *Satire* 6, the single poem which makes up Book II, provides a counterpart to this with its focus upon private life, family life and, above all, women as wives. In terms of content, then, Book II is complementary to Book I. But in terms of satiric *persona* and style it is a continuation of Book I. This explains the absence of any programmatic introduction to the Book: the programme of Book I presented in *Satire* 1 holds good for Book II.[37]

The speaker is the same angry extremist whom we met in Book I, with the addition of misogyny to his homophobia, chauvinism, and other bigotries.[38] His speech is marked by the familiar signs of indignation – angry questions, exclamations, repetition and anaphora, and sweeping exaggerations. The apparent lack of structure and sheer length of the poem also suggest someone out of control.[39] But the poem is not a rant against women; rather, it is a furious dissuasion from marriage, addressed to one Postumus who evidently ignores the speaker's advice. The course of the poem reflects his story: he leaves his bachelor state to marry, and then reaps the consequences, which include all kinds of humiliation inflicted on him by his wife, especially by her infidelity, and which culminate in death by poison at the hands of his wife.[40] The poem – which, including the 'Oxford fragment', discovered as recently as 1899,[41] is almost 700 lines long, a size unparalleled in surviving Roman satire – is on an epic scale and so fulfils the speaker's claim in Book I that satire can replace epic. That it can also replace tragedy seems 'proven' by the speaker's assertion at the end of *Satire* 6 that modern-day wives exceed the wicked wives of tragedy in their cold-bloodedness.[42]

Book III

The speaker in Books I and II is essentially an extremist and a chauvinist who sees every issue in stark black and white and becomes passionately intense in his condemnation of those who offend his simple morality. Juvenal indicates the limitations of this character by exposing the contradictions between his view of himself as a morally pure and superior being and the more objective view of him as a narrow-minded bigot. Horace had experimented with this technique in his presentation of several unimpressive fanatics in *Satires* II, of whom Damasippus (II.3) is undoubtedly the best example. Juvenal however requires more work of his audience by inviting us simultaneously to accept and reject the speaker's views. The tension provided by these contradictions is one of the sources of entertainment in these two books.

Book III (*Satires* 7–9) presents a marked shift away from the angry *persona* adopted in Books I and II, as if that *persona* had exhausted all its artistic possibilities.[43] The opening of *Satire* 7 contains no angry question or mark of indignation; in fact, the first question does not occur until lines 64–5.[44] The calm *persona* presented here is also capable of a moment of optimism concerning the prospects for poets of patronage by the emperor (1–21),[45] even if the pessimism usual in satire then takes over. Juvenal's new satiric *persona* takes a complex, double view instead of the simplistic outlook in Books I and II.[46] He deplores the lack of patronage forthcoming to intellectuals (poets, historians, orators (*causidici*), teachers of declamation (*rhetores*), and school-teachers (*grammatici*)) but at the same time, by undermining the value of their skills and expertise, suggests that these intellectuals may not deserve patronage. This is another treatment of the patron-client relationship so prominent in Book I, here with the intellectuals as the specific group of clients.[47] The treatment of the theme is a development of the angry condemnation of both patron and client in *Satire* 5: here, indignation at the humiliation given and received is replaced by a world-weary ironic detachment which deplores but accepts the conduct of both parties. The impression of a more intelligent and controlled character is enhanced by the evident structure of the poem, in which each section is clearly announced and each contains the same basic components. The fact that the topics and the order are borrowed, in inversion, from Suetonius' work *De Viris Illustribus* adds a further element of control and intellectual satisfaction.[48]

Satire 8 is the centrepiece of the Book and picks up the themes of the even-numbered poems of Book I, just as *Satires* 7 and 9 develop the odd-numbered poems. The speaker addresses to his listener, Ponticus, a persuasion to rely on one's own worth and achievements rather than on one's inheritance and line. Or, better, a dissuasion. As in *Satire* 7, the tone is essentially negative, though not without positive moments, and presents in ironically detached rather than angry tones a depressing picture of the wickedness of those who control society.[49] The theme of corruption at the centre is reminiscent of *Satires* 2 and 4, although the treatment is very different. The speaker here is a knowledgeable, experienced character, a nihilist who delights in the *reductio ad absurdum* with which the poem ends, in effect, that there is no point in relying on family trees because (272–5):

> However far back you care to go in tracing your name,
> the fact remains that your clan began in a haven for outlaws.
> The first of all your line, whatever his name may have been,
> was either a shepherd – or else a thing I'd rather not mention.

In this way, suggesting descent from criminals, he strips away from the blue-blooded but degenerate aristocrats their last resort.

Satire 9 returns to the theme of patron and client, in yet another aspect. The client in this poem is Naevolus, a man who has interpreted his duties to include satisfying the patron's homosexual needs, having sex with the patron's wife at the patron's request, and fathering the patron's children.[50] This is a development from the servility and self-humiliation accepted by the client in *Satire* 5. The client, or, rather, ex-client (he has now been rejected by his patron) attacks his former patron in a long, angry speech full of the marks of indignation which are familiar from Books I and II. But Juvenal ensures that his audience does not identify with the angry character by making the poem a dialogue (it is the only dialogue in Juvenal) between the angry Naevolus and the unnamed speaker, who clearly views Naevolus as an inferior being. This emerges in his heavy use of irony towards Naevolus, irony which is lost on Naevolus. More than ever before, then, it is the client who comes under attack in this poem. For this exploitation of irony in dialogue to discredit one of the speakers Juvenal had a fine precedent in Horace's dialogue with Catius (*Satires* II.4). He has taken this model and used it to indicate graphically that he has moved away from the angry *persona* of Books I and II by having his clever, ironic speaker in *Satire* 9 invite ridicule of the excessive anger expressed by Naevolus. Book III, then, continues the themes so familiar from Book I but uses a new cynical, ironic, and detached presentation.[51]

Books IV and V

In Book IV (*Satires* 10–12) Juvenal presents a new *persona*, which is a development from that in Book III. The new programme is declared at the beginning of *Satire* 10 where the philosophers Democritus and Heraclitus are presented as opposing models in their reactions to the world, namely laughter and tears respectively, representing detachment and involvement (lines 28–53). Of these two models, it is the Democritean which is adopted as the *persona* for Book IV while the Heraclitean is quietly abandoned.[52] Democritean tranquillity (*tranquillitas*) is mentioned explicitly as the goal of life at the end of the poem (line 364) and the same is implied in *Satires* 11 and 12.

Satire 10 is presented as a 'sermon' poem, reminiscent of Horace's diatribe satires (*Satires* I.1–3) and sermons of second-hand philosophers (*Satires* II.3, 4 and 7), on the theme of the objects and folly of prayer, perhaps best known by the title of Samuel Johnson's imitation, *The Vanity of Human Wishes*. The poem is clearly structured with sections on power (56–113), eloquence (114–32), military success (133–87), long life (188–288), and beauty (289–345). These follow an introduction (1–55) which raises the central question ('When do we have good grounds (*ratione*) for our fears or desires?'), suggests the dangers of wealth and establishes the Democritean *persona*. In each section the speaker exposes the cloud of error with which men surround themselves and at the end he gently mocks the whole process of prayer (346–53). Then he adds a list of positive suggestions of the best objects of prayer (356–62) which includes the rejection of anger, thus demonstrating how different this *persona* is from that of Books I and II. But the irreverence of the description of the act of prayer (354–5) –

> Still, that you may have something to ask for – some reason to offer
> the holy sausages and innards of a little white pig in a chapel,

the prelude to the much-quoted 'you ought to pray for a healthy mind in a healthy body' (*mens sana in corpore sano*, 356) – together with the wry tone of the ending (363–6), with its suggestion that men make things worse for themselves, both detract from the seriousness of the advice. The ending is in a very Horatian vein: Horace often closes his satirical poems with a touch of humour which makes it difficult to assess the tone of what has gone before.

Satire 11 maintains this Horatian flavour. It opens with a contradiction between two extremes of behaviour, like Horace *Satires* I.1, 2, and 3, and emphasizes knowing one's own measure, recalling Horace's stress upon the 'mean' in those and other poems.[53] With the question 'Do I practise what I preach?' at line 56 the speaker introduces the theme of self-consistency prominent in Horace *Epistles* I and, appropriately, shifts into an epistolary style. The remainder of the poem is an invitation to dinner addressed to the speaker's friend, Persicus, reminiscent in many respects of Horace *Epistles* I.5, a dinner which, in stark contrast with Juvenal's *Satire* 5, is not subject to the dictates of high fashion and allows host and guest alike the freedom to enjoy life as they choose.[54] Strongly Horatian themes of contentment, friendship, and leisure occur here, but in the unusual setting of a country meal in the city.[55] Juvenal has taken Horace's city-country antithesis and reworked it to emphasize the possibility of detachment and self-sufficiency within a city setting.

Satire 12 maintains the epistolary flavour of *Satire* 11 and develops the theme of friendship further. The bulk of the poem (1–92) describes a sacrifice offered for the safe return of a friend from near shipwreck, which incorporates a narrative in mock-epic style of the friend's danger and escape from the storm (17–82). The final section of the poem may initially appear to have little connection with the first part: it is a condemnation of legacy-hunters (the theme of Horace *Satires* II.5). But the realization that friendship is the central theme – friendship true, as shown by the speaker in his celebration of his friend's survival, and friendship false, as shown by the legacy-hunters – makes the poem coherent.[56] Moreover, if the addressee, Corvinus, of this 'letter' is himself a legacy-hunter,[57] this makes even better sense of the themes and structure of the poem.

In Book IV, then, Juvenal uses Democritus as a detached observer[58] in order to indicate the folly of human behaviour. The Book commences with a diatribe-type poem which points out man's inconsistency and it continues on that theme at the start of *Satire* 11, then shifts into the epistolary mode with a celebration of the true pleasure of friendship. The epistolary mode is continued in *Satire* 12, although it is enlarged to contain a mock-epic passage, and the theme of friendship, which was introduced in *Satire* 11, is developed here. The familiar topics of Books I–III – friendship, power, corruption, wealth – appear here but in significantly altered form. The distinctive feature of Book IV is Juvenal's blend of Horatian themes and techniques.[59]

Book V (*Satires* 13–16) presents a further development of the *persona* of Book IV. Immediately striking in *Satire* 13 is the speaker's categoric rejection of anger. The poem is a consolation addressed to Calvinus for the loss by fraud of a small sum of money. Rather, it is a mock-*consolatio*, an ironically trivial version of the standard Roman rhetorical and literary form in the event of bereavement, because the speaker shows precious little sympathy towards his addressee.[60] He explicitly condemns Calvinus' anger and his desire for vengeance (175–82). This shows how far Juvenal's *persona* has moved since Books I and II: Calvinus is now the angry man and his *indignatio* is condemned.[61] In fact, the themes of *Satire* 13 – anger, perjury, greed, and punishment – are all viewed by the speaker with an attitude of cynical detachment. He is characterized by his sense of superiority, a superiority of intellect and experience which gives him a cynically pessimistic view of mankind.

This stance of superiority is continued in *Satire* 14. The poem commences on the general theme of the bad example set by parents to their children and at 107 shifts into the particular topic of greed (*auaritia*), the only vice which is commended by parents as a virtue. The speaker's superiority emerges throughout in his knowledgeable, detached, and resigned attitude to the horrors of life and his mockery of the follies of mankind, reminiscent of the picture of Democritus' laughter in *Satire* 10.[62] But in both *Satires* 13 and 14, the frequent mention of and allusions to philosophy serve to emphasize the high intellectual status he is claiming and not to declare any particular allegiance: he is a philosopher of life.

At first sight, *Satire* 15 may seem an oddity: how does the narrative of an incident of cannibalism which took place in Egypt in a religious feud fit with *Satires* 13 and 14? Several of the themes of the poem have appeared earlier in Book V: food taboos in *Satire* 14 and religion more generally in *Satire* 13, philosophy and crime and punishment in both. But, most significantly, *Satire* 15 resumes the condemnation of anger in *Satire* 13. In *Satire* 15, anger manifests itself in a graphic form, that of murder and cannibalism – and raw cannibalism, to make it worse. The speaker condemns and despises the Egyptian tribe whose anger is not satisfied by simple murder, and he does so not with the scorn characteristic of the speaker of Books I and II but with a calmer and more detached attitude. This is shown most obviously by the fact that after the description of the atrocity (1–92) the speaker advocates a positive quality, namely *humanitas* – a concept which includes fellow-feeling, pity, a sense of community, and concord. But this positive aspect does not outweigh the speaker's cynicism, which persists to the end of *Satire* 15, where he declares that men behave worse than wild beasts (159–74).[63]

The incompleteness of *Satire* 16 prevents us from analysing its structural and thematic features. The stated programme is the advantages of military life (1–2) and in the 60 lines which survive the emphasis is on the immunity and privileges enjoyed by soldiers in legal matters, with a movement into the topic of financial advantages in the last few lines. To this extent the poem appears to continue the earlier themes of the book: crime, punishment, the courts; money, gain, and greed. How the poem continued is open to speculation.

Although Book V may at first sight seem more of a miscellany than any of the preceding books, it is unified above all by the *persona* which Juvenal here presents.[64] The speaker is superior and cynical and looks down his nose at the whole of humanity. He bears a considerable resemblance to the Democritean speaker of Book IV, but is less markedly Horatian and more philosophically eclectic. It is possible that Juvenal is here recreating a

Lucilian type of speaker. The poems of Book V handle topics which feature in Lucilius; the more lively style of Book V, while not a return to the indignation of Books I and II, is reminiscent of the variety and colour of Lucilius; and the speaker's stance of moral superiority and condescension perhaps recalls the *persona* adopted by Lucilius in his statement on *Virtus* (excellence: 1196–1208 W = 1326–38 M). This view, that Book V owes as much to Lucilius as Book IV does to Horace, must remain speculative. What is clear is that Juvenal is continually developing and modifying his satiric *persona*. The simple anger of the early *persona* (Books I and II) gives way to a more ironic view of the world which perceives two sides to any issue (Books III and IV); this ironic view finally dissolves into a superior cynicism (Book V). The condemnation of mankind in Books I and V has to some seemed similar – but Juvenal has not simply come full circle. Rather, the condemnation of mankind in Book V is delivered from a higher plane of aloofness which includes the anger of Book I as one of man's faults.

NOTES

1. Syme (1984), pp. 1120–34 is eminently judicious in his assessment of the evidence.
2. *facundus*, Mart. 7.91; see also 7.24, 12.18.
3. On the rhetorical background to the *Satires* see Kenney (1963), e.g. 707 'declamatory rhetoric, the rhetoric of the schools, is Juvenal's idiom'; Anderson (1982), pp. 396–486; and in great detail De Decker (1913).
4. The manuscripts divide the poems into five books and ancient sources who quote from the *Satires* use the same book division.

The best text of Juvenal, after the ground-breaking work of Housman (1905, second edition 1931) is Clausen's OCT (revised 1966); see now Martyn (1987). Mayor's (1886–9) and Courtney's (1980) commentaries contain a wealth of highly detailed information; more useful for the undergraduate is Ferguson (1979). None of the numerous available translations can be recommended unequivocally; Robinson (1983) sacrifices intelligibility in his faithfulness to the Latin and Rudd (1991), while a terrific improvement upon Green's widely-used Penguin, yet does not capture the rhetorical sparkle of Juvenal's Latin. Nevertheless, most of the citations included are from Rudd (1991). A useful recent publication is Ferguson's prosopography to the poems of Juvenal (1987).

All the general books on Roman satire devote substantial sections to Juvenal and provide a useful introduction to the *Satires*: Ramage, Sigsbee & Fredericks (1974), pp. 136–69; Knoche (1975), pp. 143–57; Coffey (1989), pp. 119–46 emphasizes the rhetorical elements. Mason (1963) urges that Juvenal is a poet rather than a moralist or social historian. Of the books devoted to Juvenal, Romano (1979) reflects the importance of irony as a satiric device in Juvenal's poems and Braund (1988) offers an overview of Juvenal's development of his satiric *persona* in Chapters 1 and 5. Fredericks (1979) and Bramble (1982) provide good introductions to Juvenal's most important satiric techniques, exaggeration and wit.

For further bibliography see Coffey (1963), Gérard (1976), pp. 482–510, Braund (1988), pp. 278–97.

5. Thus Waters (1970), Syme (1984), pp. 1135–57.
6. See Syme (1958), pp. 499–500, Appendices 74, 75.
7. See Braund (1988), pp. 1–23. Crucial reading on Book I is Anderson (1982), pp. 197–254, particularly on Juvenal's structural technique. On Book II see notes 37–42 below.
8. On the likely political significance of Juvenal's *indignatio* see Ramage (1989), summarized pp. 705–7.
9. Particularly Anderson (1982), pp. 293–339.

10. See previous note.
11. Only apparent; for an indication of the structure see Cloud & Braund (1982), 78–9 and below.
12. Implicit in all the *cum* clauses 22–78, in *quando* 87–9, and in *nil erit ulterius* 147.
13. On the programme presented in *Satire* 1 see Cloud & Braund (1982), 79–81.
14. On the 'Grand Style' in Juvenal's *Satires* see Scott (1927) esp. chapter 2.
15. On this theme in Juvenal Book I see LaFleur (1979).
16. Thus Kenney (1962), Griffith (1970); cf. Chapter IV note 48.
17. Thus Henderson (1989a), pp. 116–18. On deviations from the 'norm' in *Satire* 1 see Richlin (1983), pp. 195–200.
18. On Laronia's role in the poem see Braund (1988), pp. 9–11.
19. On the themes and structure of *Satire* 2 see Braund & Cloud (1981), 203–8, Wiesen (1989), 714–23.
20. On the military imagery in the poem see Anderson (1982), pp. 209–19.
21. On the relative length of the poems in Book I see Cloud & Braund (1982), 79.
22. Fredericks (1973).
23. On the symbolism of his withdrawal see Motto & Clarke (1965).
24. On the ambivalence of Umbricius see Winkler (1983), pp. 220–3, LaFleur (1976).
25. On Juvenal's theatricality here see Braund (1988), p. 15.
26. On the indignation see Sweet (1979), p. 292.
27. Editors are unanimously mistaken in their view that the mock-epic begins at 36; it clearly begins at 34 with the invocation of the muse.
28. The parody is well analysed by Anderson (1982), pp. 237–43 and Sweet (1979), esp. 288, 296.
29. On the members of the *consilium* see Highet (1954), pp. 259–61 and Vassileiou (1984), 48–59. On Juvenal's liking for such catalogues or processions, possibly inspired by Lucilius, see Griffith (1969), 147–8.
30. On the relationship between the two parts of the poem see Stegemann (1913), pp. 30–6, Helmbold & O'Neil (1956) with Kenney's strictures (1962), 30–1; Anderson (1982), pp. 232–44; Kilpatrick (1973), 230–5; Jones (1990).
31. They are preserved in Valla's note derived from the scholia now lost; cited conveniently by Highet (1954), pp. 258–9, Griffith (1969), 138, Courtney (1980), p. 195.
32. On the political overtones in *Satire* 4 see Ramage (1989), 692–704.
33. On the parallel with *Satire* 4 see Jones (1987). On the poem as a whole see Adamietz (1972), pp. 78–116, Morford (1977). Morford (1977), esp. 233–7 and 245 and Anderson (1982), pp. 244–50 provide acute analyses of the connotations of the two menus in *Satire* 5.
34. On this progressive disengagement from the client's viewpoint see Cloud & Braund (1982), 83.
35. On the structure, patterns, thematic and verbal links in the Book, including the chronological progression from *Satire* 1 to *Satire* 5, see Heilmann (1967), 366–70, Morford (1977), Cloud & Braund (1982).
36. On the highly sophisticated nature of the literary background to the *Satires* see e.g. Witke (1970), pp. 113–28 on *Satire* 1, 128–36 and Braund (1989), pp. 34–6 on *Satire* 3.
37. Thus Anderson (1982), pp. 273–4, 284, Braund (1988), p. 18.
38. On *Satire* 6 see Winkler (1983), pp. 146–206, Smith (1980). Henderson (1989a), pp. 118–22 well conveys the misogyny of the poem. On the ironic prologue to the poem see Singleton (1972).
39. On the marks of indignation and impression of incoherence see Braund (1988), pp. 18–22.
40. Most of the 'plot' of *Satire* 6 is well described by Smith (1980) who halts before the murder of the husband.
41. For arguments supporting the authenticity of the 'Oxford fragment' see Courtney (1962), Griffith (1963), Luck (1972), Martyn (1980).
42. See Bramble (1974), p. 165 and, more fully, Smith (1989). On the 'literariness' of *Satire* 6 see Wiesen (1989), 723–33.
43. On the change from Books I and II see Lindo (1974), Anderson (1982), pp. 277–92. On the invitation to reject the *persona* of Books I and II see Fredericks (1979), 185.
44. Braund (1988), p. 25. For excellent analysis of the tone of the opening 100 lines see Rudd (1976), pp. 84–118, Wiesen (1973); on the entire poem in greater detail, see Braund (1988), pp. 24–68 and, now, Hardie (1990).
45. For summary and critique of views on the opening lines see Vioni (1972–73), 242–8.
46. On the double point of view see Wiesen (1973).

47. Thus White (1978).
48. See Townend (1973), 152.
49. For an excellent introduction to the poem see Fredericks (1971a) and for detailed analysis see Braund (1988), pp. 69–129.
50. Because of its subject-matter, there is very little written specifically on *Satire* 9, despite Mason's judgement that the poem exhibits Juvenal's art 'in the purest, most concentrated form' (Mason (1963), p. 96). See Bellandi (1974); Winkler (1983), pp. 107–29; Braund (1988), pp. 130–77 for a detailed reading; Henderson (1989a), pp. 122–4 for a challenging overview. On Trebius as an intermediary stage between Umbricius and Naevolus see Bellandi (1974), 289–90; on *Satire* 5 as a forerunner to *Satire* 9 see Jensen (1981–2), 159–60; see Martyn (1970), 61 on *Satire* 9 as the climax of the themes of sexual and *clientela* perversion.
51. On the unity and structure of Book III see Braund (1988), pp. 178–83.
52. See Dick (1969), Anderson (1982), pp. 340–61; on the symbolic value of the figure of Democritus see e.g. Eichholz (1956), 65 n. 2.
53. On moderation as a theme in *Satire* 11 see Weisinger (1972); also Felton & Lee (1972).
54. For reminiscences of Horace *Epistles* I.5 see Braund (1988), p. 187. For some salutary doubts about the degree of 'friendship' between Persicus and the speaker and observations of Persicus' luxurious tastes see Jones (1983).
55. On the paradox of the country meal in the city setting see Braund (1989), pp. 46–7.
56. See Ramage (1978).
57. Thus Courtney (1980), p. 517.
58. A figure often used in satire, for example Swift's Gulliver.
59. On these features of Book IV see Braund (1988), pp. 184–9.
60. Thus Pryor (1962), Fredericks (1971b), Edmunds (1972), Morford (1973).
61. On the development from Book I see Anderson (1982), pp. 277–92.
62. See Stein (1970).
63. On the modulation between *ira* and *humanitas* in the poem see Fredericks (1976). On the speaker's unconscious betrayal of faults see McKim (1986); Anderson (1988). On the sophistication of the poem see Singleton (1983).
64. On Book V see Braund (1988), pp. 189–96.

VII. OVERVIEW OF THE GENRE

This final section offers a brief overview of the development of the genre of Roman verse satire from its origins to Juvenal and beyond with an indication of its influence on later satire. Of course, with so much of the genre missing any overview can only be provisional. I refer not only to the fragmentary preservation of the *Satires* of Ennius and Lucilius but also to the non-survival of the *Satires* of Ennius' nephew Pacuvius and, more importantly, of Turnus. Turnus was evidently a prominent satirist writing when Domitian was emperor.[1] He is quite possibly one of those referred to obliquely by Quintilian in his praise of contemporary satirists[2] and may have been a precursor to and influence upon Juvenal in adopting a declamatory mode for his satire. What other losses and absences there are from the genre of Roman verse satire can only be guessed at.

With these reservations and limitations to our overview, the genre of Roman verse satire appears to be in a process of continual development and refinement which results in an ever narrower space for the concept of satire. Beginning with the 'inventor' of the genre, it seems clear that Lucilius operated a no-holds-barred approach and embraced a wide range of material, voices and vocabulary in his *Satires*. Horace, on his own account, refined Lucilius' approach substantially, rejecting the invective associated with Lucilius in favour of laughter. In particular, he limited Lucilius' style, in general aimimg to reproduce the effect of polite discourse and in particular not permitting the use of Greek words. Yet study of Horace's poems reveals a range of themes and topics broadly similar to those treated by Lucilius. Here we find strong continuity, with a significant element of refinement of the genre chiefly in the area of stylistics.

The next stage is Persius. Just as Horace was immersed in Lucilius,[3] so Persius was immersed in Horace[4] — and, doubtless, Lucilius, although this is harder to substantiate given the fragmentary state of the text of Lucilius. In the *Satires* of Persius we see many of the themes and forms used by his predecessors in the genre, but of the many varied voices presented in Horace only a few survive, most obviously that of the philosophical fanatic. Persius' most significant contribution to the genre is the graphic language and imagery used by the fiercely independent *persona* he presents. This stage, too, then, represents a narrowing of the genre, although in the case of Persius this may be due partly to the fact that he wrote only one book;

had he lived to complete this book and to compose others, he may well have exhibited a greater variety and developed the genre further.

The fierce voice of Persius reappears in the early *Satires* of Juvenal in his creation of an angry *persona*. The genre has by now moved a long way from the genteel and gentlemanly tones of Horace's *Epistles*, although there is still a substantial overlap in the themes which feature. These tones do not return, not even in Juvenal's later *Satires* in which he abandons anger for an ironic, nihilistic, and cynical voice unparalleled in Horace.

After Juvenal, satire is chiefly associated with anger and aggression.[5] It seems that Juvenal's own limitation of the genre, particularly in his early *Satires*, established this central characteristic for all subsequent authors. And once satire was viewed simply as the angry unmasking of faults and vices it became acceptable to Christians and was a type of writing well represented in the Middle Ages.[6] What is noticeable in this period is a relaxation of the strict rules of genre which applied during the Roman era. There is a development away from a particular literary form – the hexameter verse satire – to a satiric tone or spirit available within a diversity of forms.[7]

The same holds true for subsequent practitioners of satire in languages other than Latin, including English. Satire denotes a tone rather than a specific form. There are exceptions to this generalization. Poets of the Elizabethan and Jacobean period, including John Donne, John Marston, and Joseph Hall, present a type of formal verse satire which is clearly heavily influenced by the classical satirists.[8] What is remarkable is that, despite their evident familiarity with the works of Horace, it is the aggressive tone associated with Persius and Juvenal which they adopt. In the development of the genre, then, the progressive refinement and limitation in scope seen in Roman verse satire continued as satire passed into other languages and literatures. But at the same time a movement in the opposite direction can also be seen, as the concept of a genre with strict rules disappeared, satire widened to denote, simply, a fiercely critical tone of voice.[9] And this remains true today: any modern definition of satire emphasizes tone rather than form and content. What we have to remember when we read the Roman verse satirists is that all three elements were important. Here lies a challenge for the modern reader: if we make the effort to understand the framework within which the Roman satirists were working, we gain a deeper appreciation of the diversity and inventiveness of their poetry.

NOTES

1. On Turnus see Coffey (1979).
2. Quintilian *I.O.* 10.1.94, quoted above in Chapter II.
3. As shown above all by Fiske's study (1920).
4. Thus Rudd (1976), pp. 54–83.
5. On Greek and Roman satire after Juvenal see Ramage, Sigsbee & Fredericks (1974), pp. 170–6.
6. On this phenomenon see Classen (1988).
7. Thus Ramage, Sigsbee & Fredericks (1974), pp. 175–6, naming Theodulf of Orléans (eighth-ninth century), Hugh Primas of Orléans and Walter of Châtillon (twelfth century); for detailed analysis of these three medieval exponents of Latin satire see Witke (1970), pp. 168–266.
8. On the formal verse satire in English Renaissance writers and later see Randolph (1942).
9. For a brief survey of some Renaissance and modern satire see Ramage, Sigsbee & Fredericks (1974), pp. 176–83.

BIBLIOGRAPHY

ADAMIETZ, J. (1972): *Untersuchungen zu Juvenal*, Hermes Einzelschriften 26 (Wiesbaden).
ANDERSON, W. S. (1982): *Essays on Roman Satire* (Princeton).
ANDERSON, W. S. (1988): 'Juvenal Satire 15: Cannibals and Culture', in *The Imperial Muse: Ramus Essays on Roman Literature of the Empire. To Juvenal Through Ovid*, ed. A. J. Boyle (Berwick, Victoria, Australia), pp. 203–14.
ARMSTRONG, D. (1964): 'Horace, *Satires* I,1–3: A Structural Study', *Arion* 3, 86–96.
ARMSTRONG, D. (1970): 'Two Voices of Horace', *Arion* 9, 91–112.
ARMSTRONG, D. (1986): '*Horatius Eques et Scriba*: Satires 1.6 and 2.7', *TAPhA* 116, 255–88.
ARMSTRONG, D. (1989): *Horace* (New Haven and London).
BELLANDI, F. (1974): 'Naevolus Cliens', *Maia* 26, 279–99.
BOLL, F. (1913): 'Die Anordnung im zweiten Buch von Horaz' Satiren', *Hermes* 48, 143–5.
BOND, R. P. (1978): 'A Discussion of Various Tensions in Horace, *Satires* 2.7', *Prudentia* 10, 85–98.
BOND, R. P. (1985): 'Dialectic, Eclectic and Myth (?) in Horace, *Satires* 2.6', *Antichthon* 19, 68–86.
BOND, R. P. (1987): 'The Characterisation of the Interlocutors in Horace, *Satires* 2.3', *Prudentia* 19, 1–21.
BRAMBLE, J. C. (1974): *Persius and the Programmatic Satire* (Cambridge).
BRAMBLE, J. C. (1982): 'Martial and Juvenal', in *The Cambridge History of Classical Literature II: Latin Literature* edd. E. J. Kenney & W. V. Clausen (Cambridge), pp. 597–623.
BRIND'AMOUR, L. & P. (1971): 'La deuxième satire de Perse et le *dies lustricus*', *Latomus* 30, 999–1024.
BRAUND, S. H. (1988): *Beyond Anger: A Study of Juvenal's Third Book of Satires* (Cambridge).
BRAUND, S. H. (ed.) (1989): *Satire and Society in Ancient Rome* (Exeter), including 'City and Country in Roman Satire', pp. 23–47.
BRAUND, S. H. & CLOUD, J. D. (1981): 'Juvenal: A Diptych', *LCM* 6, 195–208.
BRINK, C. O. (1963): *Horace on Poetry: Prolegomena to the Literary Epistles* (Cambridge).
BRINK, C. O. (1971): *Horace on Poetry: The 'Ars Poetica'* (Cambridge).
BRINK, C. O. (1982): *Horace on Poetry: Epistles Book II* (Cambridge).
BUCHHEIT, V. (1968): 'Homerparodie und Literaturkritik in Horazens Sat. I 7 und I 9', *Gymnasium* 75, 519–55.
BUSHALA, E. W. (1971): 'The motif of sexual choice in Horace, *Satire* 1.2', *CJ* 66, 312–15.
CHRISTES, J. (1972): 'Lucilius. Ein Bericht über die Forschung seit F. Marx (1904/5)', in *ANRW* I.2, 1182–1239.
CLASSEN, C. J. (1973): 'Eine unsatirische Satire des Horaz? Zu Hor. sat. I.5', *Gymnasium* 80, 235–50.

CLASSEN, C. J. (1978): 'Horace – a cook?', *CQ* 28, 333–48.
CLASSEN, C. J. (1988): 'Satire – The Elusive Genre', *SO* 63, 95–121.
CLAUSS, J. J. (1985): 'Allusion and Structure in Horace Satire 2.1: The Callimachean Response', *TAPhA* 115, 197–206.
CLOUD, J. D. (1989): 'Satirists and the Law', in *Satire and Society in Ancient Rome* ed. S. H. Braund, pp. 49–67.
CLOUD, J. D. & BRAUND, S. H. (1982): 'Juvenal's Libellus – A Farrago?', *G&R* 29, 77–85.
COFFEY, M. (1963): 'Juvenal Report for the Years 1941–1961', *Lustrum* 8, 161–215.
COFFEY, M. (1979): 'Turnus and Juvenal', *BICS* 26, 88–94.
COFFEY, M. (1989): *Roman Satire*² (Bristol).
CONINGTON, J. (1874): *The Satires of A. Persius Flaccus*, ed. H. Nettleship, 2nd ed. Oxford, 3rd ed. 1893, repr. 1967 (Hildesheim).
CONNOR, P. (1988): 'The Satires of Persius: A Stretch of the Imagination', in *The Imperial Muse: Ramus Essays on Roman Literature of the Empire. To Juvenal Through Ovid*, ed. A. J. Boyle (Berwick, Victoria, Australia), pp. 55–77.
COSTA, C. D. N. (ed.) (1973): *Horace* (London and Boston).
COURTNEY, E. (1962): '*Vivat ludatque cinaedus*', *Mnemosyne* 15, 262–6.
COURTNEY, E. (1980): *A Commentary on the Satires of Juvenal* (London).
CURRAN, L. (1970): 'Nature, Convention, and Obscenity in Horace, Satires 1.2', *Arion* 9, 220–45.
DAWSON, C. M. (1950): 'The Iambi of Callimachus. A Hellenistic Poet's Experimental Laboratory', *YCS* 11, 1–168.
DECKER, J. DE (1913): *Juvenalis Declamans: Etude sur la Rhétorique Déclamatoire dans les Satires de Juvénal* (Ghent).
DESSEN, C. S. (1968): '*Iunctura Callidus Acri*': *A Study of Persius' Satires* (Urbana, Chicago and London).
DEWITT, N. W. (1935): 'Parresiastic Poems of Horace', *CPh* 30, 312–19.
DICK, B. F. (1969): 'Seneca and Juvenal 10', *HSCP* 73, 237–46.
DICKIE, M. (1981): 'The Disavowal of *Invidia* in Roman Iamb and Satire', in *Papers of the Liverpool Latin Seminar Third Volume*, ed. F. Cairns (Liverpool), pp. 183–208.
DILKE, O. A. W. (1973): 'Horace and the Verse Letter', in *Horace*, ed. C. D. N. Costa, pp. 94–112.
DUQUESNAY, I. M. LE M. (1984): 'Horace and Maecenas: The propaganda value of *Sermones* I', in *Poetry and Politics in the Age of Augustus*, edd. T. Woodman & D. West (Cambridge), pp. 19–58.
EDMUNDS, L. (1972): 'Juvenal's Thirteenth Satire', *RhM* 115, 59–73.
EICHHOLZ, D. E. (1956): 'The Art of Juvenal and his Tenth *Satire*', *G&R* 3, 61–9.
ELLIOTT, R. C. (1960): *The Power of Satire: Magic, Ritual, Art* (Princeton).
FEINBERG, L. (1963): *The Satirist* (Ames, Iowa).
FELTON, K. & LEE, K. H. (1972): 'The Theme of Juvenal's Eleventh Satire', *Latomus* 31, 1041–6.
FERGUSON, J. (1979): *Juvenal. The Satires* (New York).
FERGUSON, J. (1987): *A Prosopography to the Poems of Juvenal* (Brussels).
FISKE, G. C. (1909): 'Lucilius and Persius', *TAPhA* 40, 121–51.
FISKE, G. C. (1913): 'Lucilius, the Ars poetica of Horace, and Persius', *HSCP* 24, 1–36.
FISKE, G. C. (1920): *Lucilius and Horace* (Madison, repr. 1970 Westport).

FLINTOFF, E. (1982): 'Food for Thought. Some imagery in Persius Satire 2', *Hermes* 110, 341–54.
FRAENKEL, E. (1957): *Horace* (Oxford).
FREDERICKS, S. C. (1971a): 'Rhetoric and Morality in Juvenal's 8th Satire', *TAPhA* 102, 111–32.
FREDERICKS, S. C. (1971b): 'Calvinus in Juvenal's Thirteenth Satire', *Arethusa* 4, 219–31.
FREDERICKS, S. C. (1973): 'The Function of the Prologue (1–20) in the Organisation of Juvenal's Third Satire', *Phoenix* 27, 62–7.
FREDERICKS, S. C. (1976): 'Juvenal's Fifteenth Satire', *ICS* 1, 174–89.
FREDERICKS, S. C. (1979): 'Irony of Overstatement in the Satires of Juvenal', *ICS* 4, 178–91.
FRISCHER, B. (1991): *Shifting Paradigms. New Approaches to Horace's Ars Poetica* (Georgia).
FRYE, N. (1944): 'The Nature of Satire', *University of Toronto Quarterly* 14, 75–89.
FRYE, N. (1957): *Anatomy of Criticism: Four Essays* (Princeton).
GÉRARD, J. (1976): *Juvénal et la Réalité Contemporaine* (Paris).
GRATWICK. A. S. (1982): 'Lucilius', in *The Cambridge History of Classical Literature II: Latin Literature*, edd. E.J.Kenney & W.V.Clausen (Cambridge), pp.162–71.
GRIFFITH, J. G. (1963): 'The Survival of the Longer of the So-called Oxford Fragments of Juvenal's Sixth Satire', *Hermes* 91, 104–14.
GRIFFITH, J. G. (1969): 'Juvenal, Statius, and the Flavian Establishment', *G&R* 16, 134–50.
GRIFFITH, J. G. (1970): 'The Ending of Juvenal's First Satire and Lucilius, Book XXX', *Hermes* 98, 56–72.
GRIMES, S. (1972): 'Structure in the Satires of Persius', in *Neronians and Flavians. Silver Latin I*, ed. D. R. Dudley (London and Boston), pp. 113–54.
HAIGHT, E. H. (1947): 'Menander at the Sabine Farm, "Exemplar Vitae"', *CPh* 42, 147–55.
HALLETT, J. P. (1981): '*Pepedi / diffissa nate ficus*: Priapic Revenge in Horace *Satires* I.8', *RhM* 124, 341–7.
HARDIE, A. (1990): 'Juvenal and the condition of letters: the Seventh Satire', in *Papers of the Leeds International Latin Seminar Sixth Volume*, ed. F. Cairns (Leeds), pp. 145–209.
HARRISON, G. (1987): 'The Confessions of Lucilius (Horace Sat. 2.1.30–34): A Defense of Autobiographical Satire?', *Classical Antiquity* 61, 38–52.
HARVEY, R. A. (1981): *A Commentary on Persius* (Leiden).
HEILMANN, W. (1967): 'Zur Komposition der vierten Satire und des ersten Satirenbuches Juvenals', *RhM* 110, 358–70.
HELMBOLD, W. C. & O'NEIL, E. N. (1956): 'The Structure of Juvenal IV', *AJPh* 77, 68–73.
HENDERSON, J. G. W. (1989a): ' ... when Satire writes "Woman"', in *Satire and Society in Ancient Rome*, ed. S. H. Braund, pp. 89–125.
HENDERSON, J. (1989b): 'Satire writes "woman": Gendersong', *PCPhS* 35, 50–80.
HENDRICKSON, G. L. (1897): 'Are the Letters of Horace Satires?', *AJPh* 18, 313–24.
HENRICKSON, G. L. (1928): 'The First Satire of Persius', *CPh* 23, 97–112.
HIGHET, G. (1954): *Juvenal the Satirist* (Oxford).
HIRTH, H. J. (1985): *Horaz, der Dichter der Briefe. Rus und Urbs* (Hildesheim).
HODGART, M. (1969): *Satire* (Verona).
HOOLEY, D. (1984): '*Mutatis mutandis*: Imitations of Horace in Persius' First Satire', *Arethusa* 17, 81–95.
HUDSON, N. A. (1989): 'Food in Roman Satire', in *Satire and Society in Ancient Rome*, ed. S. H. Braund, pp. 69–87.
HUNTER, R. L. (1985): 'Horace on Friendship and Free Speech', *Hermes* 113, 480–90.

JENKINSON, R. (1973): 'Interpretations of Persius', Satires 3 and 4', *Latomus* 32, 521–49.
JENKINSON, J. R. (1980): *Persius: The Satires* (Warminster).
JENSEN, B. FRUELUND (1981–82): 'Crime, vice and retribution in Juvenals' Satires', *C&M* 33, 155–68.
JONES, F. (1983): 'Towards an Interpretation of Juvenal Satire 11', *AClass* 26, 104–7.
JONES, F. M. A. (1987): 'Trebius and Virro in Juvenal 5', *LCM* 12, 148–54.
JONES, F. M. A. (1990): 'The persona and dramatis personae in Juvenal Satire Four', *Eranos* 88, 47–59.
KENNEY, E. J. (1962): 'The First Satire of Juvenal', *PCPhS* 8, 29–40.
KENNEY, E. J. (1963): 'Juvenal: Satirist or Rhetorician?', *Latomus* 22, 704–20.
KERNAN, A. (1959): *The Cankered Muse: Satire of the English Renaissance* (New Haven).
KILPATRICK, R. S. (1973): 'Juvenal's "Patchwork" Satires: 4 and 7', *YCS* 23, 229–241.
KILPATRICK, R. S. (1986): *The Poetry of Friendship: Horace Epistles I* (Edmonton).
KILPATRICK, R. S. (1989): *The poetry of criticism: Horace, Epistles II* (Edmonton).
KISSEL, W. (1981): 'Horaz 1936–1975: Eine Gesamtbibliographie', in *ANRW* II.31.3, 1403–1558.
KNOCHE, U. (1975): *Roman Satire* tr. E. S. Ramage (Bloomington and London).
KORZENIEWSKI, D. (1970): 'Die erste Satire des Persius', in *Die römische Satire*, ed. D. Korzeniewski (Darmstadt), pp. 384–438.
LAFLEUR, R. A. (1976): 'Umbricius and Juvenal Three', *Ziva Antika* 26, 383–431.
LAFLEUR, R. A. (1979): '*Amicitia* and the Unity of Juvenal's First Book', *ICS* 4, 158–77.
LAFLEUR, R. A. (1981): 'Horace and *Onomasti Komodein*: The Law of Satire', in *ANRW* II.31.3, 1790–1826.
LEACH, E. W. (1971): 'Horace's *Pater Optimus* and Terence's Demea: Autobiographical Fiction and Comedy in *Sermo*, I.4', *AJPh* 92, 616–32.
LEE, G. & BARR, W. (1987): *The Satires of Persius* (Liverpool).
LINDO, L. I. (1974): 'The Evolution of Juvenal's Later Satires', *CPh* 69, 17–27.
LUCK, G. (1972): 'The Textual History of Juvenal and the Oxford Lines', *HSCP* 76, 217–32.
LUDWIG, W. (1968): 'Die Komposition der beiden Satirenbucher des Horaz', *Poetica* 2, 304–25.
MCGANN, M. J. (1954): 'Horace's Epistle to Florus (Epist. 2.2)', *RhM* 97, 343–58.
MCGANN, M. J. (1969): *Studies in Horace's First Book of Epistles* (Brussels).
MCGANN, M. J. (1973): 'The Three Worlds of Horace's Satires', in *Horace*, ed. C. D. N. Costa, pp. 59–93.
MCKEOWN, J. C. (1979): 'Augustan Elegy and Mime', *PCPhS* 25, 71–84.
MCKIM, R. (1986): 'Philosophers and Cannibals: Juvenal's Fifteenth Satire', *Phoenix* 40, 58–71.
MACLEOD, C. (1979): 'The Poetry of Ethics: Horace *Epistles* I', *JRS* 69, 16–27 (= *Collected Essays* 1981 Oxford, pp. 280–91).
MARTIN, J. M. K. (1939): 'Persius – Poet of the Stoics', *G&R* 8, 172–82.
MARTYN, J. R. C. (1966): 'Imagery in Lucilius', in *Wissenschaftliche Zeitschrift der Universität Rostock, Römische Satire* 15, 493–505.
MARTYN, J. R. C. (1970): 'A New Approach to Juvenal's First *Satire*', *Antichthon* 4, 53–61.
MARTYN, J. R. C. (1979): 'Juvenal's Wit', *Grazer Beiträge* 8, 219–38.
MARTYN, J. R. C. (1980): 'Further Evidence on Juvenal's Oxford Fragments', *Scriptorium* 34, 247–53.

MARTYN, J. R. C. (1987): *D.IVNI IVVENALIS SATVRAE* (Amsterdam).
MARX, F. (1904-5): *C.Lucilii Carminum Reliquiae Vols. I & II* (Leipzig).
MASON, H. A. (1963): 'Is Juvenal A Classic?', in *Critical Essays on Roman Literature: Satire*, ed. J. P. Sullivan, pp. 93-176.
MAYER, R. (1985): 'Horace on good manners', *PCPhS* 31, 33-46.
MAYER, R. (1986): 'Horace's *Epistles* I and Philosophy', *AJPh* 107, 55-73.
MAYOR, J. E. B. (1886-89): *Thirteen Satires of Juvenal*[4] (London and Cambridge).
MERWIN, W. S. (1981): *The Satires of Persius* (London).
MOLES, J. (1985): 'Cynicism in Horace *Epistles* 1', in *Papers of the Liverpool Latin Seminar, Fifth Volume*, ed. F. Cairns, pp. 33-60.
MORFORD, M. (1973): 'Juvenal's Thirteenth Satire', *AJPh* 94, 26-36.
MORFORD, M. (1977): 'Juvenal's Fifth Satire', *AJPh* 98, 219-45.
MORFORD, M. (1984): *Persius* (Boston).
MOTTO, A. L. & CLARKE, J. R. (1965): 'Per iter tenebricosum. The Mythos of Juvenal 3', *TAPhA* 96, 267-76.
MUECKE, F. (1979): 'Horace the Satirist: Form and Method in *Satires* I.4', *Prudentia* 11, 55-68.
NISBET, R. G. M. (1963): 'Persius', in *Satire*, ed. J. P. Sullivan, pp. 39-71.
OLTRAMARE, A. (1924): *Les Origines de la Diatribe Romaine* (Geneva).
PORT, W. (1926): 'Die Anordnung in Gedichtbüchern augusteischer Zeit', *Philologus* 81, 280-308, 427-68.
PRYOR, A. D. (1962): 'Juvenal's False Consolation', *Journal of the Australasian Universities Language and Literature Association* 18, 167-80.
PUELMA-PIWONKA, M. (1949): *Lucilius und Kallimachos. Zur Geschichte einer Gattung der hellenistich-römischen Poesie* (Frankfurt).
RAMAGE, E. S., SIGSBEE, D. L., & FREDERICKS, S. C. (1974): *Roman Satirists and Their Satire* (New Jersey).
RAMAGE, E. S. (1978): 'Juvenal, Satire 12: On Friendship True and False', *ICS* 3, 221-37.
RAMAGE, E. S. (1989): 'Juvenal and the Establishment: Denigration of Predecessor in the "Satires"', in *ANRW* II.33.1, 640-707.
RANDOLPH, M. C. (1942): 'The Structural Design of the Formal Verse Satire', *PhQ* 21, 368-84.
RASCHKE, W. J. (1979): 'The Chronology of the Early Books of Lucilius', *JRS* 69, 78-89.
RASCHKE, W. J. (1987): '*Arma pro amico* - Lucilian Satire at the Crisis of the Roman Republic', *Hermes* 115, 299-318.
RASCHKE, W. J. (1990): 'The Virtue of Lucilius', *Latomus* 49, 352-69.
RECKFORD, K. J. (1962): 'Studies in Persius', *Hermes* 90, 476-504.
RECKFORD, K. J. (1969): *Horace* (New York).
RICHLIN, A. (1983): *The Garden of Priapus. Sexuality and Aggression in Roman Humor* (New Haven and London).
RICHLIN, A. (1984): 'Invective Against Women in Roman Satire', *Arethusa* 17, 67-80.
ROBERTS, M. (1984): 'Horace *Satires* 2.5: Restrained Indignation', *AJPh* 105, 426-33.
ROBINSON, S. (1983): *Juvenal: Sixteen Satires Upon the Ancient Harlot* (Manchester).
ROMANO, A. C. (1979): *Irony in Juvenal* (Hildesheim).
RUDD, N. (1957): '*Libertas* and *Facetus*', *Mnemosyne* 10, 319-36.
RUDD, N. (1966): *The Satires of Horace* (Cambridge).
RUDD, N. (1976): *Lines of Enquiry: Studies in Latin Poetry* (Cambridge).

RUDD, N. (1982): 'Persius', in *The Cambridge History of Classical Literature II: Latin Literature*, edd. E.J.Kenney & W.V.Clausen (Cambridge), pp. 503–10.
RUDD, N. (1986): *Themes in Roman Satire* (London).
RUDD, N. (1987): *Horace: Satires and Epistles. Persius: Satires* (Harmondsworth).
RUDD, N. (1989): *Horace Epistles Book II and Epistle to the Pisones ('Ars Poetica')* (Cambridge).
RUDD, N. (1991): *Juvenal. The Satires* (Oxford).
RUTHERFORD, R. B. (1981): 'Horace, *Epistles* 2.2: Introspection and Retrospective', *CQ* 31, 375–80.
SCODEL, R. (1987): 'Horace, Lucilius, and Callimachean polemic', *HSCP* 91, 199–215.
SCOTT, I. G. (1927): *The Grand Style in the Satires of Juvenal* (Northampton, Mas.).
SHACKLETON BAILEY, D. R. (1982): *Profile of Horace* (London).
SHERO, L. R. (1922): 'The Satirist's *Apologia*', *Wisconsin Studies in Language and Literature* 15, 369–78.
SHERO, L. R. (1923): 'The *Cena* in Roman Satire', *CPh* 18, 126–43.
SINGLETON, D. (1972): 'Juvenal 6.1–20, and Some Ancient Attitudes to the Golden Age', *G&R* 19, 151–65.
SINGLETON, D. (1983): 'Juvenal's Fifteenth Satire: A Reading', *G&R* 30, 198–207.
SMITH, W. S., JR. (1980): 'Husband vs. Wife in Juvenal's Sixth Satire', *CW* 73, 323–32.
SMITH, W. S. (1989): 'Heroic Models for the Sordid Present: Juvenal's View of Tragedy', in *ANRW* II.33.1, 811–23.
SQUILLANTE SACCONE, M. (1985): 'La poesia di Persio alla luce degli studi più recenti (1964–1985)', in *ANRW* II.32.3, 1781–1812.
STEGEMANN, W. (1913): *De Iuvenalis Dispositione* (Weidae Thuringorum).
STEIN, J. P. (1970): 'The Unity and Scope of Juvenal's Fourteenth Satire', *CPh* 65, 34–7.
SULLIVAN, J. P. (ed.) (1963): *Critical Essays on Roman Literature, Vol. II: Satire* (London).
SULLIVAN, J. P. (1972): 'In Defence of Persius', *Ramus* 1, 48–62.
SULLIVAN, J. P. (1985): *Literature and Politics in the Age of Nero* (Ithaca, N.Y.).
SWEET, D. (1979): 'Juvenal's Satire 4: Poetic Uses of Indirection', *California Studies in Classical Antiquity* 12, 283–303.
SYME, R. (1958): *Tacitus* (Oxford).
SYME, R. (1984): *Roman Papers III*, ed. A. R. Birley (Oxford).
TOWNEND, G. B. (1973): 'The Literary Substrata to Juvenal's Satires', *JRS* 63, 148–60.
VAHLEN, J. (1963): *Ennianae Poesis Reliquiae*³ (Amsterdam).
VAN ROOY, C. A. (1965): *Studies in Classical Satire and Related Literary Theory* (Leiden).
VAN ROOY, C. A. (1968): 'Arrangement and Structure of Satires in Horace, *Sermones*, Book I, with more special reference to Satires 1–4', *AClass* 11, 38–72.
VAN ROOY, C. A. (1970a): 'Arrangement and Structure of Satires in Horace, *Sermones*, Book I: Satires 4 and 10', *AClass* 13, 7–27.
VAN ROOY, C. A. (1970b): 'Arrangement and Structure of Satires in Horace, *Sermones*, Book I: Satires 5 and 6', *AClass* 13, 45–59.
VAN ROOY, C. A. (1971): 'Arrangement and Structure of Satires in Horace, *Sermones*, Book I: Satire 7 as related to Satires 10 and 8', *AClass* 14, 67–90.
VAN ROOY, C. A. (1972a): 'Arrangement and Structure of Satires in Horace, *Sermones*, Book I: Satires 9 and 10', *AClass* 15, 37–52.
VAN ROOY, C. A. (1972b): 'Horace, *Sat*. I,1 and I,6 and the Topos of Cardinal Vices', *Antidosis (Festschrift W. Kraus), Wiener Studien Beiheft* 5, pp. 297–305.

VAN ROOY, C. A. (1973): '"Imitatio" of Vergil, *Eclogues* in Horace, *Satires*, Book I', *AClass* 16, 69–88.
VASSILEIOU, A. (1984): 'Crispinus et les conseillers du prince (Juvénal, *Satires*, IV)', *Latomus* 43, 27–68.
VIONI, G. (1972–73): 'Considerazione sulla settima satira di Giovenale', *Rendiconti dell'Accademia delle Scienze dell'Istituto di Bologna* 61, 240–71.
WARMINGTON, E. H. (1956): *Remains of Old Latin Vol. 1* (London).
WARMINGTON, E. H. (1979): *Remains of Old Latin Vol. 3* (London).
WASZINK, J. H. (1963): 'Das Einleitungsgedicht des Persius', *WS* 76, 79–91.
WATERS, K. H. (1970): 'Juvenal and the Reign of Trajan', *Antichthon* 4, 62–77.
WEISINGER, K. (1972): 'Irony and Moderation in Juvenal XI', *California Studies in Classical Antiquity* 5, 227–40.
WEST, D. (1967): *Reading Horace* (Edinburgh).
WEST, D. (1974): 'Of Mice and Men: Horace, *Satires* 2.6.77–117', in *Quality and Pleasure in Latin Poetry*, edd. T. Woodman & D. West (Cambridge), pp. 67–80.
WHITE, P. (1978): '*Amicitia* and the Profession of Poetry in Early Imperial Rome', *JRS* 68, 74–92.
WIESEN, D. S. (1973): 'Juvenal and the Intellectuals', *Hermes* 101, 464–83.
WIESEN, D. S. (1989): 'The Verbal Basis for Juvenal's Satiric Vision', in *ANRW* II.33.1, 708–33.
WILLIAMS, G. (1968): *Tradition and Originality in Roman Poetry* (Oxford).
WILLIAMS, G. (1972): *Horace* (Oxford).
WINKLER, M. M. (1983): *The Persona in Three Satires of Juvenal* (Hildesheim).
WITKE, C. (1970): *Latin Satire: The Structure of Persuasion* (Leiden).
ZETZEL, J. E. G. (1980): 'Horace's *Liber Sermonum*: The Structure of Ambiguity', *Arethusa* 13, 59–77.